CHRISTIAN LIFE
GOD'S WAY

LARRY HARMSEN

ISBN 978-1-63575-939-6 (paperback)
ISBN 978-1-63575-940-2 (digital)

Christian Faith Publishing, Inc.
832 Park Avenue
Meadville, PA 16335
www.christianfaithpublishing.com

Unless otherwise indicated, Scripture quotations are from the English Standard Version (ESV).

Printed in the United States of America

CONTENTS

PREFACE

The chapters in this book are not sequential in nature. Each chapter is a separate Bible study, some completed as long ago as 30 years, and some completed recently, and most in between those times. The order of each chapter is intended to have the potential to carry the reader into a closer intimacy with our Lord and Savior because of, hopefully, gaining greater knowledge and understanding of the Bible. I hope and pray that it does so with you; to God be the glory.

Although I study in the King James Version, the English Standard Version is used in Bible quotes, as it is considered a literal version and is easy to read.

February 7, 2019
Author

1

IS GOD TRUSTWORTHY?

Is God a liar?

Is God faithful?

Is God dependable?

Is God trustworthy?

Does God really love me?

Romans 8:28 states, "And we know that for those who love God all things work together for good, for those who are called according to his purpose."

That verse doesn't say that all things are good, and it doesn't mean that all things are good. It means that for those who love God, to them who are the called according to His purpose, God does make everything *work together* for good. At the very least, it means that the person who loves God, who is among the *called according to His purpose*, is going to learn more about God's love and power, thereby becoming stronger in faith (it may take years). That person will be on the way to a closer walk with God, and will be able to be more used by God.

When suffering mental anguish or physical hurt, prove your own salvation.

Galatians 6:4 states, "But let each one test his own work, and then his reason to boast will be in himself alone and not in his neighbor."

Second Corinthians 13:5 states, "Examine yourselves, to see whether you are in the faith. Test yourselves. Or do you not realize this about yourselves, that Jesus Christ is in you?—unless indeed you fail to meet the test!"

What is the proof? Is the Holy Spirit working in your life to draw you closer to Christ in His Word and in your own righteousness?

> For all who are led by the Spirit of God are sons of God. For you did not receive the spirit of slavery to fall back into fear, but you have received the Spirit of adoption as sons, by whom we cry, "Abba! Father!" The Spirit himself bears witness with our spirit that we are children of God,… Likewise the Spirit helps us in our weakness. For we do not know what to pray for as we ought, but the Spirit himself intercedes for us with groanings too deep for words. And he who searches hearts knows what is the mind of the Spirit, because the Spirit intercedes for the saints according to the will of God. And we know that for those who love God all things work together for good, for those who are called according to his purpose. For those whom he foreknew he also predestined to be conformed to the image of his Son, in order that he might be the firstborn among many brothers. And those whom he predestined he also called, and those whom he called he also justified, and those whom he justified he also glorified (Rom. 8:14–16, 26–30).

Jeremiah 29:11 states, "For I know the plans I have for you, declares the LORD, plans for wholeness and not for evil, to give you a future and a hope." God wants nothing except the best for you. But none of us know what is the best for us. God tells us that it is best for us to know Him, first in salvation, then in close personal relationship. He tells us that it is best for us to do things His way, Joshua 24:15 states, "And if it is evil in your eyes to serve the LORD, choose this day whom you will serve, whether the gods your fathers served in the region beyond the River, or the gods of the Amorites in whose land you dwell. But as for me and my house, we will serve the LORD." Read Deuteronomy 28 to see what will happen if we do not chose to serve God with our actions, thoughts, time, and worship.

First Corinthians 10:13 states, "No temptation has overtaken you that is not common to man. God is faithful, and he will not let you be tempted beyond your ability, but with the temptation he will also provide the way of escape, that you may be able to endure it."

Each and every Christian has the grace available to escape temptation. The question is, "Do you want to tap into the power of grace to use it?"

Isaiah 55:8–9 states, "For my thoughts are not your thoughts, neither are your ways my ways, declares the LORD. For as the heavens are higher than the earth, so are my ways higher than your ways and my thoughts than your thoughts."

God is always aware of what is going to happen and what is happening and what has happened. Yes, He very often does not keep some things from happening. Why? Because it is for the best! We don't think so, but He knows so. We may think He is wrong. But He is never wrong! He is *perfect.*

Possibly the unexpected death of a loved one is merely to keep something worse from happening. But it has other reasons than that too.

    a. He wants us to know Him better. Hebrews 4:15–16 states, "For we do not have a high priest who is unable to sympathize with our weaknesses, but one who in every respect has been tempted as we are, yet without sin. Let us then with confidence draw near to the throne of grace, that we may receive mercy and find grace to help in time of need."

    b. Loved ones learn to lean on Christ. Proverbs 3:5–6 states, "Trust in the LORD with all your heart, and do not lean on your own understanding. In all your ways acknowledge him, and he will make straight your paths."

c. A loved one is being prepared to be used by God. Psalms 126:5–6 states, "Those who sow in tears shall reap with shouts of joy! He who goes out weeping, bearing the seed for sowing, shall come home with shouts of joy, bringing his sheaves with him" (going forth, weeping, bearing precious seed, means that, while suffering, when we go forth to serve others [bearing precious seed] we will receive the grace to rejoice; both serving and rejoicing leads to healing).

d. If we just let God be God, we also will be faced with the decision to trust, or not to trust. Luke 20:17–18 states, "But he looked directly at them and said, "What then is this that is written: 'The stone that the builders rejected has become the cornerstone'"? Everyone who falls on that stone will be broken to pieces, and when it falls on anyone, it will crush him." Falling upon the stone means to let God be God in our lives, accepting Him in faith and trust. The person on whom the stone falls is the person who refuses to let God be God in their life. If applied to a Christian, God will then discipline that person.

> And have you forgotten the exhortation that addresses you as sons? 'My son, do not regard lightly the discipline of the Lord, nor be weary when reproved by him. For the Lord disciplines the one he loves, and chastises every son whom he receives.' …For the moment all discipline seems painful rather than pleasant, but later it yields the peaceful fruit of righteousness to those who have been trained by it. Therefore lift your drooping hands and strengthen your weak knees, and make straight paths for your feet, so that what is lame may not be put out of joint but rather be healed.(Heb 12:5–6, 11–13).

The discipline will either lead to a greater trust in Him, or it will lead to mental or physical destruction, based upon our own decision to either live in His grace or to not live in His grace.

Know that our lives have a purpose. Ephesians 2:8–10 states, "For by grace you have been saved through faith. And this is not your own doing; it is the gift of God, not a result of works, so that no one may boast. For we are his workmanship, created in Christ Jesus for good works, which God prepared beforehand, that we should walk in them."

We need to take personal responsibility for our own life before God. Romans 12:1–2 states, "I appeal to you therefore, brothers, by the mercies of God, to present your bodies as a living sacrifice, holy and acceptable to God, which is your spiritual worship. Do not be conformed to this world, but be transformed by the renewal of your mind, that by testing you may discern what is the will of God, what is good and acceptable and perfect."

John 14:12–14 states, "Truly, truly, I say to you, whoever believes in me will also do the works that I do; and greater works than these will he do, because I am going to the Father. Whatever you ask in my name, this I will do, that the Father may be glorified in the Son. If you ask me anything in my name, I will do it."

This does not mean that God will answer any prayer that we ask of Him. It says, if we ask anything *in His Name*. We hear that, and say that, without really knowing what it means. What does *In His Name* really mean? It means whatever meets the standards of who He is, in His perfection, righteousness, purity, and holiness. It means that if we pray His perfect will, it will be done. What is His perfect will? If we are not close to Him, we won't know it. We will only know it by grace, living a life with no unforgiven sin, yielding to Him in everything, including our own desires and wants. Then He can put His will into us, and we can pray His will, and He will answer that prayer. John 15:7 states, "If you abide in me, and my words abide in you, ask whatever you wish, and it will be done for you."

All of the above passages point toward one thing. We were created to honor Him, which can only be done by submitting to Him and letting Him work through us. Then He will bear fruit in and through us, and we will earn crowns of victory to cast at Jesus feet. Only in this way will we really find joy and fulfillment in this life.

2

GRACE & FAITH

We have all heard of *grace*. And most of us have heard the verses that are in this study. But have we really put the verses and teaching of grace together for a more full understanding? My study on *grace* really started about twenty-five years ago, when I did a word study on *grace*. It went into deep study about fifteen years ago when I started to meditate on why some people who thought they were saved never displayed even the slightest evidence of salvation, and other people who were new converts displayed immediate evidence of salvation, and everything in between. It has been my burden of joy, given by God, empowered by grace, to find the truth, using only the Bible. This study is the result of years of living by grace and years of Bible study.

In this study, I intend to cover several things.

- The definition of *grace*, including some Bible passages using the word *grace*.

- The purpose and use of grace in our own personal walk with our Lord. In this section, we will also look at what biblical righteousness is.

- The purpose and use of grace in our walk in this world, as the light of the Lord. In this section, we will look at what *agape* love is and how it relates to grace.

Psalms 84:11 states, "For the LORD God is a sun and shield; the LORD bestows favor and honor. No good thing does he withhold from those who walk uprightly."

Definition of *grace* – transliterated *charis* means favor given without expectation of return. It is most often translated grace (130 times in the New Testament). It is translated "favor" six times. And it is translated using other words just a few times.

Some passages about grace used in ways other than the focus of this study.

- Luke tells us that Mary, the mother of Jesus, "have found favor with God" (Luke 1:30). The word *favor* is the Greek word for grace.

- Luke also gives us a small picture of the childhood of Jesus. Luke 2:40, 52 (emphasis added) states, "And the child grew and became strong, filled with wisdom. And the *favor* of God was upon him… And Jesus increased in wisdom and in stature and in *favor* with God and man." (The word *favor* is actually the word *grace*).

Grace may also mean gracefulness in movement, speech and elegance in relationships, although it is not used this way in the Bible.

Grace may also mean words of love and intent. When Jesus began His ministry, he read from the Old Testament in a synagogue and started to exposit on the passage. He had quoted Isaiah 61:1 when He read, "The Spirit of the Lord is upon me, because he has anointed me to proclaim good news to the poor. He has sent me to proclaim liberty to the captives and recovering of sight to the blind, to set at liberty those who are oppressed, to proclaim the year of the Lord's favor" (Luke 4:18-19). The Bible tells us, in Luke 4:22, "And all spoke well of him and marveled at the *gracious* words that were coming from his mouth. And they said, 'Is not this Joseph's son?'"

The word *gracious* is the word *grace*. The words of Jesus were also graceful in that they not only caught the hearer but had tremendous meaning in fulfillment of Scripture through Himself. There was great power here, but the people could not bring themselves to pay attention to the power of God. Most of the common people of Jesus' day were blind to who He was because they had preconceived ideas of who He was. The spiritual leaders of His day could not see who He was, because they had faulty ideas of what the Old Testament said and because they loved the power of being in positions of authority. The question must be asked, "Do we really understand Jesus?" *If we don't understand what the Bible teaches about grace, we will never understand Jesus in the way He wants us to.*

We all know that salvation is by grace. Ephesians 2:8–9, which many of us memorized when we were children in Sunday school, says, "For by grace you have been saved through faith. And this is not your own doing; it is the gift of God, not a result of works, so that no one may boast."

I will also look at some other aspects of grace in the Bible. This will not be an exhaustive study on grace. But I have stated several times in the past that I think *grace* is the most important word in the Bible, regarding not only salvation but the life and living of the Christian who desires to follow Christ.

We will find out that grace is very important to the life of the Christian. Grace is not just receiving God's free gift of salvation. Grace is the power and direction of every aspect of the life of *every* Christian.

DOES GRACE HELP WHEN WE ARE WEAK?

We Christians live knowing right from wrong and trying our best not to do wrong. We try to live a life pleasing to God, by what we do, or what we don't do, what we think or don't think, what we say or don't say. We think and reason our way through a decision to make and decide this is the right way. And then we do what we have decided.

Is that good? Or is it bad? It depends upon our attitude. Maybe we are doing good for prideful reasons; no one sees that our thoughts are actually bad.

If we have made a lifestyle of doing what we think is best, in our own eyes, using what we have learned in the Bible, we are actually living under our own power. We are living by our own freewill. We live a life of goodness because we have made that our choice. We have chosen not to do bad. And that is good. But is it best? Is God pleased that we are not doing wrong? Yes, but is that all He expects from us?

What about when we, as Christians, don't have the will to do good? Everyone has something that controls him or her. It could be laziness, self-centeredness, gambling, stealing, hatred, pride, sex, or any of the things called vices. Paul had some weakness that he called a thorn in his side. We know that he had some kind of disease in his eyes (Gal. 4:14–15). But I think that he was talking about something else, like one of the vices, rather than something physical. He could not always control it on his own; rather, it wanted to control him. God purposely did not tell us what that weakness was. We may be wrong when we try to discover what the weakness is by misinterpreting parts of the Bible. God told us that Paul had a weakness. I don't think any of us, except maybe the proud, would deny that each one of us has a weakness that we are ashamed of and that quite often compromises our Christian walk with our Lord.

Second Corinthians 12:7–9a (emphasis added) states, "So to keep me from being conceited by the surpassing greatness of the revelations, a thorn was given me in the flesh, a messenger of Satan to harass me, to keep me from being conceited. Three times I pleaded with the Lord about this, that it should leave me. But he said to me, 'My grace is sufficient for you, for my power is made perfect in weakness.'" It seems that the thorn in his side may be pride, as he said, in two places, "to keep me from being conceited." Paul then goes on to say in v. 12b, *"Therefore I will boast all the more gladly of my weaknesses, so that the power of Christ may rest upon me."*

When that weakness of vice fights with our sense of righteousness, what do we do? We fight back. And sometimes, maybe most of the time, we lose. And we hate ourselves for failing ourselves and

God. We pray about it, asking God to forgive us and take that weakness of ours away. And we fail again. And we pray again. And we fail again. And after a while, we get hardened about it and don't fight it so much, and just accept that evil activity of ours. And not only are we affected, but our family, friends, and local church are also affected. Yes, you are surprised! Your local church? Of course. God knows what's going on. It is sin in the local church, and God doesn't like it. So He withholds blessings from the church because of our sin. Why do you think our local churches are so ineffective in so many ways?

> Let not sin therefore reign in your mortal bodies, to make you obey their passions. Do not present your members to sin as instruments for unrighteousness, but present yourselves to God as those who have been brought from death to life, and your members to God as instruments for righteousness. For sin will have no dominion over you, since you are not under law but under grace (Rom. 6:12–14).

It is useless to try to gain victory in our Christian life by doing things under our own power, our own freewill, even when it seems like we are successful.

Paul puts it this way, in Romans 7:14–19:

> For we know that the law is spiritual, but I am of the flesh, sold under sin. I do not understand my own actions. For I do not do what I want, but I do the very thing I hate. Now if I do what I do not want, I agree with the law, that it is good. So now it is no longer I who do it, but sin that dwells within me. For I know that nothing good dwells in me, that is, in my flesh. For I have the desire to do what is right, but not the ability to carry it out. For I do not do the good I want, but the evil I do not want is what I keep on doing.

Paul said that even though he was a Christian, he often did not do good when he knew it was right to do good, and that he did wrong when he knew it was wrong. Why? Because he was living by his own freewill in making his decisions, rather than allowing God to live through him by grace.

In Romans 11:4–6 (emphasis added), Paul is discussing the Jews as God's chosen people. Some thought that God had cast the Jews away (Covenant Theology). Paul answered what God had told Elijah after Jezebel had threatened his life:

> But what is God's reply to him? "I have kept for myself seven thousand men who have not bowed the knee to Baal." So too at the present time there is a remnant, *chosen by grace*. But if it is by grace, it is no longer on the basis of works [meaning our own efforts of freewill]; otherwise grace would no longer be grace.

God makes a very distinct difference between doing things under our own power, our own thinking of what is right and good, acting by our own will, or by God working in and through us by grace. If we are being right in our own eyes, then we are still under the law, by which it is impossible to please God. If we are by God's power, denying our self in humility before God, submitting to Him in everything, letting Him guide us in what is right in His eyes, then we are living by grace.

Galatians 5:25 states, "If we live by the Spirit, let us also keep in step with the Spirit." That means to walk in and by grace.

God has given us that better way. Paul said in 2 Corinthians 12:9, "My grace is sufficient for you: for my power [strength] is made perfect in weakness." God's grace was sufficient for Saul, the great Persecutor of the Faith, whom God renamed Paul, that great Hero of the Faith. Surely God's grace is sufficient for each Christian. God's strength is made perfect in weakness. That does not mean that God's strength is made perfect through our failures (although, hopefully, we learn from them). It does mean that when we rely upon God's grace to take us through our Christian life, *we will win*. We will live a victorious Christian life because through the power of God's grace working in us, our strength, which is weak in itself, is made perfect by grace. Our weakness is made strong by God's grace! Philippians 4:13 states, "I can do all things through him who strengthens me."

What about when we are in our own strength? What if we know we are working for God, by our own strength, by our own freewill? Unfortunately, if our own freewill is not crushed and purged out of us, we are weaker than when we are weak in Christ's grace. John 15:2 states, "Every branch of mine that does not bear fruit he takes away [more correctly, lifts up to clean and tie in place so it can receive light from the sun (Son)], and every branch that does bear fruit he prunes, that it may bear more fruit." We can't do God's will in our weakness without Christ's grace. We can't even do God's will in our own strength. It is only when we put our own desires aside and take Christ's desires as our own and act upon them by God's power (grace) that we can do His will. And none of this can be done by our own freewill. It is only possible by grace! God wants us to live every part of every day this victorious way! John 10:10b states, "I came that they may have life and have it abundantly." We have a choice that sometimes is a difficult choice to make. We can live by our own freewill, or we can live by God's grace, each and every second of every day of our lives.

To live by God's grace means that we cannot live in our own self-centeredness. We have to empty ourselves of self-centeredness. The Bible means that when it says that we have to die daily.

> For through the law I died to the law, so that I might live to God. I have been crucified with Christ. It is no longer I who live, but Christ who lives in me. And the life I now live in the flesh I live by faith in the Son of God, who loved me and gave himself for me. I do not nullify the grace of God, for *if righteousness were through the law, then Christ died for no purpose.* (Gal. 2:19–21; emphasis added)

What is Paul saying here? We Christians are exhorted to be dead to the Law, which is doing what we think is right by our own efforts, our own freewill. Paul means that to work by our own freewill to do what we think is right should be dead in the Christian. Instead, we are to let God, by His grace, live in us and through us, putting His own desires in us, to do what God knows is right. When we do that, we are actually righteous, because God, by His grace, is doing the work, not we, by our own freewill. Paul exhorted us to *not* frustrate the grace of God, because if being righteous by our own power were possible, then Christ's death was in vain. In other words, it is absolutely impossible for us to be righteous by our own freewill. For Paul, everything in a Christian's life is either worked by God's grace or worked by our own freewill. There is no other option, no other choice. Paul chose grace. What is our choice?

WHAT IS ACTUAL RIGHTEOUSNESS IN THE CHRISTIAN?

What is actual or biblical righteousness? Paul said in Romans 8:3–4 (emphasis added), "For God has done what the law, weakened by the flesh, could not do. By sending his own Son in the likeness of sinful flesh and for sin, he condemned sin in the flesh, in order *that the righteous requirement of the law might be fulfilled in us, who walk not according to the flesh but according to the Spirit.*"

First of all, all Christians have had righteousness imputed to them at salvation. "Imputed" is a financial term that means to put into an account, like a bank account. In this passage, imputed righteousness means that although we are sinful, wicked, spiritually dirty and unacceptable to God in any manner, the perfection, or righteousness, of Jesus Christ stands in our place before God the Father. Instead of seeing you, me, or any other Christian, God the Father chooses to see the perfect sacrifice of Jesus Christ in our place. So the righteousness of Jesus Christ is standing in the place of our sinful selves before God, which is the only way that He can accept us into His fellowship. He is such a holy, righteous, perfect God that nothing that is not absolutely perfect or righteous can be in His presence. Because we are not righteous, we cannot be completely righteous until our rapture into heaven. The righteousness of Jesus Christ, which stands in our place before God, is imputed righteousness. Every Christian is in good standing before God, being acceptable in His presence by that imputed righteousness. But there is more. Imputed righteousness is not what is meant in Romans 8:4 (emphasis added), where it said, "that the righteousness requirement of the law might be *fulfilled* in us, who *walk not according to the flesh, but according to the Spirit.*" Paul is talking about actual righteousness in us.

God freely imputes righteousness to our spiritual account. But He expects more from us. He expects us to be actually righteous. He expects us to be Christ-like. He gave us, and is still giving us, the ability to be Christ-like, to be actually righteous.

> May grace and peace be multiplied to you in the knowledge of God and of Jesus our Lord. His divine power has granted to us all things that pertain to life and godliness, through the knowledge of him who called us to his own glory and excellence, by which he has granted to us his precious and very great promises, *so that through them you may become partakers of the divine nature, having escaped from the corruption that is in the world because of sinful desire.* (2 Pet. 1:2–4; emphasis added)

This passage is talking about experiencing grace by living in grace and being actually righteous by grace. We can be righteous by grace.

Romans 3:10 states, "as it is written: 'None is righteous, no, not one;...'" So how can we be Christ-like? How can be we actually righteous? Only by the miracle of grace working in us.

> But thanks be to God, that you who were once slaves of sin have become obedient from the heart to the standard of teaching to which you were committed, and, having been set free from sin, have become slaves of righteousness. I am speaking in human terms, because of your natural limitations. For just as you once presented your members as slaves to impurity and to lawlessness leading to more lawlessness, so now present your members as slaves to righteousness leading to sanctification (Rom. 6:17–19).

Paul is telling us, "having been set free from sin, [we] have become slaves of righteousness." There are a several dynamics in this sentence given below, phrase by phrase:

- "Having been set free from sin." This is the imputed righteousness. It is passive voice, meaning that God caused this to happen, not the person.

- [We] "have become slaves of righteousness." This means that we must be continually yielded to grace. We are yielded, in that we put aside our freewill and started living by grace. This, also, is passive voice, meaning that God caused this to happen by grace, not the person by his or her own will.

- As we started living by grace, we started a life of obedience to God. In that obedience, we started to become actually righteousness. This is active voice (our own choice and action). Because of living in Grace, we were able to obey.

The particular word *righteousness* in verse 19 and many other places in the Bible means to meet the standards that are set by the person who has the right and authority to create those standards. In other words, it means to live up to the standards of perfection that God has set for all people, as is reflected by His own holiness. But only those who are covered by the death and resurrection of Jesus Christ, through imputed righteous, can do that in a passive, not active way. This is exactly why the nonbeliever will go to hell for eternity and why we believers will go to be with God for eternity. It is very important to understand that we cannot define for ourselves what righteousness is. God and only God can do that.

To be acceptable to God in our thoughts and actions, we need to be servants (slaves) of righteousness. We do that by yielding our members, as given in Romans 12:1–2: "I appeal to you therefore, brothers, by the mercies of God, to present your bodies as a living sacrifice, holy and acceptable to God, which is your spiritual worship. Do not be conformed to this world, but be transformed by the renewal of your mind, that by testing you may discern what is the will of God, what is good and acceptable and perfect." But how do we do that? By our own freewill? Impossible! It takes the work of God by grace.

In Romans 12:1–2, we see several things:

- "Present your bodies as a living sacrifice, holy and acceptable unto God, which is your spiritual worship." God appeals, beseeches (KJV) us to offer ourselves to Him. The words Paul used point directly to the Old Testament sacrifice offered to God. Those sacrifices were killed. Paul said that in sacrificing ourselves to God, we do it while living, and we keep on living as long as God keeps us here on this earth. Galatians 2, verses 20 and 21 adds some New Testament wisdom: "I have been crucified with Christ. It is no longer I who live, but Christ who lives in me. And the life I now live in the flesh I live by faith in the Son of God, who loved me and gave himself for me. I do not nullify the grace of God, for if justification were through the law, then Christ died for no purpose."

- "Do not be conformed to this world." This means an act of our will to refute the carnality of the world. A better way is to lay aside our own freewill and take upon ourselves the will of our Master. We can't do this without the next step.

- "be transformed by the renewal of your mind." This means to take upon ourselves the will of our Master by total submission, yielding to Him, and being willing to live by His grace, which is God working in and through us, to perform His will. That willingness to live by His grace can happen only by His grace.

Grace is the power of God, through love, given to us to do His will. It is only by grace that we can become servants of righteousness.

We learn to become righteous by Grace. Is that all there is for Grace to do? Or does God want us, in righteousness, to lead others closer to Christ in our interactions with them, by Grace?

To answer that, let's look at love. This love, transliterated *agape,* is self-sacrificial love. It is the love that Romans 5:8 tells us about: "But God shows us his love for us in that while we were still sinners, Christ died for us." *Agape* love is motivated to do one thing, and one thing only. It is to draw people closer to Christ, first in salvation, and then in spiritual growth and maturity (sanctification), learning to live the Christian life, or to live a Christ-like life. God's *agape* love in action is grace. Grace is God's power, by His *agape* love, offered to everyone who ever lived, first for salvation, and after salvation, to sanctification, Christian growth and maturity, living a life pleasing to God and beneficial to His people. That is what John wrote about in John 10:10b: "I came that they may have life and have it abundantly."

Grace is very simply, God's agape love in action, empowered by the Holy Spirit.

- Grace is the power of God that enabled our salvation.

  o Ephesians 2:8–9 states, "For by grace you have been saved through faith. And this is not your own doing; it is the gift of God, not a result of works, so that no one may boast."

- Grace is a new life in Christ.

  o Second Corinthians 5:17 states, "Therefore, if anyone is in Christ, he is a new creation. The old has passed away; behold, the new has come."

- Grace is the power of God to change our lives to be more Christ-like.

  o Acts 20:32 (emphasis added) states, "And now I commend you to God and to *the word of his grace*, which is able to build you up and to give you the inheritance among all those who are sanctified."

- Grace is being the light of the world.

  o Second Corinthians 5:18–21 states, "All this is from God, who through Christ reconciled us to himself and gave us the ministry of reconciliation; that is, in Christ God [the Father] was reconciling the world to himself, not counting their trespasses against them, and entrusting to us the message of reconciliation. Therefore, we are ambassadors for Christ,

God making his appeal through us. We implore you on behalf of Christ, be reconciled to God. For our sake he made him to be sin who knew no sin, so that in him we might become the righteousness of God.

- Grace is having the heart of God.
  - Isaiah 55:8–9 states, "For my thoughts are not your thoughts, neither are your ways my ways, declares the LORD. For as the heavens are higher than the earth, so are my ways higher than your ways and my thoughts than your thoughts."
  - First Timothy 2:4 states that God, "desires all people to be saved and to come to the knowledge of the truth…"
  - First John 2:10 states, "Whoever loves his brother abides in the light, and in him there is no cause for stumbling."
  - First John 3:16 states, "By this we know love, that he laid down his life for us, and we ought to lay down our lives for the brothers."
  - Philippians 2:5–7, "Have this mind among yourselves, which is yours in Christ Jesus, who, though he was in the form of God, did not count equality with God a thing to be grasped, but emptied himself, taking the form of a servant, being born in the likeness of men."
- Grace, built upon the doctrine of the Word, is the foundation of Christian living.
  - Philippians 4:12–13 states, "I know how to be brought low, and I know how to abound. In any and every circumstance, I have learned the secret of facing plenty and hunger, abundance and need. I can do all things through him who strengthens me." Paul is talking about grace here. Through grace, Paul knows how to abound and how to suffer need.

By grace, he can do all things through Christ which strengthens him. The Greek root word of strengthen is where we get the word dynamite from. It is exceedingly strong power. The word in Philippians 4:13 *strengthen* means to enable with that dynamite power. Pretty powerful concept here!

A clarification is appropriate at this time. Salvation is not an act of our will. People will tell you that salvation is by grace, but they will also tell you that it is an act of freewill. That is biblical heresy. It is impossible if the Bible is taken literally. Salvation is a miracle of the love of God in our being. It cannot, biblically, be explained in any way, except that it is a miracle of grace. People of God, that is exactly what grace is. Grace is the miraculous work of God in us. I will quote Spiros Zodhiates, pg. 1469 of *The Complete Wordstudy Dictionary New Testament*, under Strong's #5485, which is transliterated *charis*, translated as *grace*.

- Zodhiates writes that *charis* (grace) stands in direct antithesis to Strong's #2041, transliterated *ergon*, translated as works, the two being mutually exclusive."

Where do "works" come from? "Works" come from freewill. Grace and freewill are mutually exclusive. They cannot coexist. It is impossible for grace and freewill to work together. Matthew 9:16–17 states, "No one puts a piece of unshrunk [new, unwashed] cloth on an old garment, for the patch tears away from the garment, and a worse tear is made. Neither is new wine put into old wineskins. If it is, the skins burst and the wine is spilled and the skins are destroyed. But new wine is put into fresh wineskins, and so both are preserved."

Grace is the miraculous work of God, working in and through us, by God's love, to do His will. It is God's work, not our own. It is grace, not freewill.

That is what it means to live in the Spirit, living by grace, instead of living in the flesh, which is by freewill. Romans 8:1–17 is about this (not recorded here, as it is a long passage, but is well worth reading). We are not talking about unsaved people here. We are talking about saved people, Christians. Every person can have only one lord, either Jehovah God through God the Son, or Satan. Yes, a saved person can have Satan as his or her lord some or most of the time.

- Romans 6:16 states, "Do you not know that if you present yourselves to anyone as obedient slaves, you are slaves of the one whom you obey, either of sin, which leads to death, or of obedience, which leads to righteousness?"

- Matthew 6:24 states, "No one can serve two masters, for either he will hate the one and love the other, or he will be devoted to the one and despise the other. You cannot serve God and money."

- John 6:44, 65, "No one can come to me unless the Father who sent me draws him. And I will raise him up on the last day... And he said, 'This is why I told you that no one can come to me unless it is granted him by the Father.'"

Whenever a Christian is not empowered by the miracle of grace, thereby living in the Spirit, he or she is honoring Satan, who is then that person's lord. Only when we live by grace, walking in the Spirit, can we honor our true God as God. You may ask, "Can we have Satan as lord even when we are doing the things God said, in His Word, to do?" Yes, even when we think we are doing God's will. You may be driving down the road, thinking, even willing yourself that you are going south. But if you are going north, you are thinking wrong. Many, many Christians are doing wrong, thinking they are pleasing God. And God sends messengers to set them straight. But they don't hear, because they have hardened their heart against anything that does not agree with what they want to be right, or what they have heard in local church meetings that don't fully understand God's precious Word to us (1 Tim. 3:16–17)!

THE UNBELIEVER AND GRACE

But, back to God's self-sacrificial love and grace, leading to salvation, you may ask, "What about those who are not saved?"

God's love is extended to everyone.

- First Timothy 2:4 states that God "desires all people to be saved and to come to the knowledge of the truth."

- Second Peter 3:9 states, "The Lord is not slow to fulfill his promise as some count slowness, but is patient toward you, not wishing that any should perish, but that all should reach repentance."

God's grace, the power to do God's will, is offered to everyone. We like to think that God, in His sovereignty, is all-powerful and can do anything. He is all powerful, but He cannot, or will not, do just anything. He is limited by His nature or by limiting His power. In God's nature, He is a moral God, unlike the (false) gods of mythology, which I believe are based upon reality (see Gen. 6:1–2 and Jude 6; Numbers 13:21–22; 1 Sam. 17) which would include Goliath and his brothers and sons, some of whom David's mighty men killed. The first of the Ten Commandments commands, "You shall have no other gods before me." (Exodus 20:3). Jehovah God, God the Son and God the Holy Spirit, our true God, the Holy Trinity, is a moral God. He cannot do anything that denies His own nature. He cannot do anything except what He determined to be perfectly and morally righteous, and He never changes (Numbers 23:19; First Samuel 15:29; Malachi 3:6; Romans 11:29; Titus 1:2; James 1:17). He also created people to share Himself with, people who would love, honor, and worship Him, not because they have to but because they want to. In that desire of God's, He created freewill, which was perfect when He created it. But He knew that freewill would not stay perfect. Because God created free will, He limited Himself regarding freewill. He will not tread on it. He does not want to have fellowship with robots who would do anything He told them to do in perfect obedience. He does want to have fellowship with people who choose to do what He tells them to do. But, since the fall, that was impossible. Grace has filled the gap of impossibility, but if the grace is rejected or ignored by freewill, He will not interfere. The insistence of free will, bringing the absence of grace brings eternal damnation.

God's default, regarding those with whom He will have fellowship with, is for a person to be overcome by the awesome, miraculous power of grace, thereby being yielded to God. But anyone who resists that grace, by exercising freewill, cannot become saved. Grace and freewill, as noted before, are opposites. They are incompatible. They cannot coexist. Freewill will conquer Grace, not because it is stronger but because God will not interfere with it, so that we could choose either self or God.

Grace, when not rejected, softens our hearts for salvation. That is the beginning work of grace. Salvation cannot be done by our own choice, as we are incapable of choosing it. It is all God's work, none of our own (Ephesians 2:8–9). We either accept God by not rejecting grace (which is only by grace), or we reject grace by asserting our freewill against the saving "dynamite" action of grace.

Let's take a close look at John 3:16–18:

> "For God so loved the world, that he gave his only Son, that whoever believes in him should not perish but have eternal life. For God did not send his Son into the world to condemn the world, but in order that the world might be saved through him. Whoever believes in him is not condemned, but whoever does not believe is condemned already, because he has not believed in the name of the only Son of God.

Look at verse 18: "Whoever believes in him is not condemned, but whoever does not believe is condemned already, because he has not believed in the name of the only Son of God."

The Greek speaking person will understand this to say, "He that believes on Jesus Christ, not by his or her own action, but by the action of God, the Father, is not condemned. This is in the passive voice, meaning that God, not the person, did the action. The person only received the action.

But he or she that chooses, by his or her own freewill, not to believe on Jesus Christ as Savior, condemns his or her own self by that choice of freewill, and is condemned already, because of his or her own choice not to believe in the name of the only begotten Son of God. This is because the tense is in the middle voice, which means that the person who, in the active tense, rejects the salvation of God (by rejecting grace), he or she receives the result of that action. In the middle voice, that person caused, by choice, the action, which was rejection of grace by freewill. So, in effect, the person caused his or her own condemnation because of the action of freewill. God does not condemn a person to hell just because of what some people falsely call predestination. A person condemns him- or herself to hell by resisting grace by free choice, or freewill. God has set the judgment of eternity in hell for those who resist the grace of salvation. But He does not choose who will go to hell. That choice is made by each person who rejects grace.

There are only two choices for the believer or for the unbeliever: receive grace, by not rejecting it (which is totally God's work), or reject grace, which is by freewill.

APPLICATION FOR GRACE

God left us here, on earth, after salvation, so that we can be a light upon a hill, the light that exposes darkness and enlightens people of the Savior and brings salvation. That light that shines through us, when we let it, is grace. It is the dynamite power of God to bring salvation to the unsaved, and to draw people closer to Him in spiritual growth. It is undeserved, unmerited favor. It is receiving what we don't deserve. It is the opportunity, given by Christ, to be used by us, Christians. It is bearing fruit. It is being safe in the Righteous Right Hand of God (Eccl. 9:1).

Please look at these verses from the book of Ephesians, each of which have the word *grace*. Think about what each means, in the light of what has been taught here, before going on to the next verse.

Ephesians 1:2 states, "Grace to you and peace from God our Father and the Lord Jesus Christ."

Ephesians 1:6–7 states, "to the praise of his glorious grace, with which he has blessed us in the Beloved. In him we have redemption through his blood, the forgiveness of our trespasses, according to the riches of his grace."

Ephesians 1:5,2:7–8 states, "...he predestined us for the adoption to himself as sons through Jesus Christ according to the purpose of His will,…so that in the coming ages he might show the immeasurable riches of his grace in kindness toward us in Christ Jesus, For by grace you have been saved through faith. And that not of your own doing; it is the gift of God."

Ephesians 3:2,7–8 states, "assuming that you have heard of the stewardship of God's grace that was given to me for you,… Of this gospel I was made a minister according to the gift of God's grace, which was given me by the working of his power. To me, though I am the very least of all the saints, this grace was given, to preach to the Gentiles the unsearchable riches of Christ."

Ephesians 4:7 states, "But grace was given to each one of us according to the measure of Christ's gift."

Ephesians 4:29 states, "Let no corrupting talk come out of your mouths, but only such as is good for building up, as fits the occasion, that it may give grace to those who hear."

Ephesians 6:24 states, "Grace be with all who love our Lord Jesus Christ with love incorruptible."

There are many more verses in the Bible that tell us about grace. Here are a few:

> Romans 5:1–2 states, "Therefore, since we have been justified by faith, we have peace with God through our Lord Jesus Christ. Through him we have also obtained access by faith into this grace in which we stand, and we rejoice in hope of the glory of God."

> First Corinthians 12:4–7 states, "Now there are varieties of gifts (grace), but the same Spirit; and there are varieties of service, but the same Lord; and there are varieties of activities, but it is the same God who empowers them all in everyone. To each is given the manifestation of the Spirit for the common good."

Grace is the basis of everything we do that gives honor to our Lord and Savior. Freewill is the basis of everything that we do that does not give Him honor. Only what is done by God's grace is sufficient to count as righteousness.

GRACE AND LOVE

The love of God, the love of John 3:16, described in the love chapter (1 Cor. 13), given to us at salvation, is *agape* (noun) or *agapeo* (verb). God gave His people this love, which is not known in the carnal world. He gave it to us to return to Him and to exercise it on others. *Agape* love always involves personal investment, or to put it another way, a*gape* love always comes with sacrifice. It could be giving of time, dispensing wisdom, just being with someone, giving of money or goods, or other things. It can only be exercised in drawing a person to Christ or drawing a person closer to Christ. Contrary to what many people think, this love is not emotional but is a decision of the will. That is not to say that *agape* love can't involve emotion; it should! But it should never be an emotional work; it must be an act of the will. Grace is the same way. Emotions may lead to exercising grace, but the decision to act should involve our own personal decision of the will to act, driven by and empowered by God's grace. Grace is God's love in action, and we should be emotional about God's love in action, for it is the greatest power on earth!

Grace always involves self-sacrifice. The sacrificial atonement of Jesus Christ involved great personal sacrifice. He suffered greatly, physically, emotionally, and spiritually, to do God's will so that we could be saved. In Philippians 2:6–8, we find the *kenosis*, the "self emptying of Christ." While never ceasing to be God, He "emptied" Himself of being God so that He could be completely, 100 percent human so that He would do the work by which we are saved. He did the work that we are incapable of doing! For the Christian, the work of that *agape* love in and through us should also involve an emptying of self-centered freewill, taking upon ourselves God's will and making that our own will. *Agape* love always does God's will, which is, in general (not all-inclusive), found in John 3:16; First Timothy 2:4; Second Peter 3:9; 2 Timothy 2:15; Ephesians 1:15-23; Ephesians 4; Ephesians 5:17–20; 1 John 3; and the Ten Commandments; and First Corinthians 13:1. And there are so many other passages and principles that we could document here, but it all comes down to this: God's grace, as well as God's *agape / agapeo* love, has one purpose, which is to draw people to Him, first in salvation, and then in a life relationship with Him. The purpose He gave us is to do His will and to worship Him, which includes learning and understanding Scripture, living a life pleasing to Him, and becoming fully devoted to Him, all of which lead and enable us to lead others into that same relationship with Him, by the grace (power) of God's love, God's Word and the Holy Spirit. Love is a decision of the will.

SYNOPSIS OF GRACE

The description of grace, according to my studies of the Bible, is that

- Grace is God's love in action.

- Grace always involves the Holy Spirit, who works through the Word. This is why it is so important to spend time in the Bible and prayer every day! Note that the Greek word for grace is transliterated *charis*, pronounced "khar'-ece." The Greek word for the work of the Holy Spirit, often translated "spirituals" or "gifts" or "spiritual gifts" is transliterated *charisma*. The connection of these two words is obvious. For context, see 1 Corinthians 12:4, 9.

- Grace always involves the Word of God, which is the boundary within which grace works. Grace always works the will of God and never works against the will of God. You will find that the same applies to God's *agape* love, which He gives to us at salvation.

- Grace can be, and often is, rejected or ignored. God created mankind with perfect freewill. But the freewill of mankind, through Adam and Eve, compromised that freewill to the point that no person who ever existed, or ever will exist, other than Jesus Christ, can do God's will by our own compromised freewill, without that freewill being influenced and led by Grace (Ephesians 5:18; Colossians 3:16). Freewill, without grace, can only lead a person away from God, never to God. Grace, on the other hand, will always lead a person to God or closer to God, never away from God. As such, grace and freewill are opposed to each other. Please note that this is not discussing an unsaved person as compared to a Christian. This is talking about an unsaved person and a Christian living by his or her own freewill as compared to a Christian living by submitting his or her own desires to God and accepting God's grace to work His will. Pay very close attention to Matthew 6:24: "No one can serve two masters, for either he will hate the one and love the other, or he will be devoted to the one and despise the other. You cannot serve God and money [worldly goods or values]." See God's directions to Israel (Deuteronomy 30:15–18); Joshua's exhortation to Israel (Joshua 24:14–15); Eli and his sons (1 Samuel 2:29–30); David and Bathsheba (2 Samuel 11–12); and Roman 8.

- When grace, the work of God through His love, through His Word, through the Holy Spirit, is not rejected or ignored, grace is the *active* part of reception by the person. The person is always passive. It is God's work. God gets the glory. The person receives the grace passively so that he or she cannot boast of the achievements that grace brings (Ephesians 2:8–9); that glory belongs only to God.

- Grace is the energy, or the power, that empowers a Christian to do God's will. When the Christian works by grace, God is much pleased; it is God's expectation that the Christian will always be dominated by grace: Ephesians 4:17 through 5:20, especially verse 5:18, "But be filled with the Spirit."

I know that parts of the above description of grace are very difficult to understand and accept, but it will become plain by the end of this book, so hang on. This description of grace is what it means when the Bible says, "but be filled with the Spirit" (Ephesians 5:18c).

Romans 11:6 states, "But if it is by grace, it is no longer on the basis of works; otherwise grace would no longer be grace." The word *work* or *works* means any effort on our own part by our own will. In other words, God's grace and our own efforts are opposite of each other; they cannot work together and they cannot coexist. They cannot both be present at salvation! The Bible teaches that salvation occurred because God showered that person with grace and the grace was not rejected or ignored (which is only by Grace!). Note what is stated here. *The spiritual baptism, salvation, did not take place because the grace of God was accepted!* It took place because the grace was *not rejected or ignored!* There is a difference here. If salvation by the grace of God was actively accepted on our part (which can only be by the effort of freewill), the person involved would have "worked" for his or her salvation, which the Bible absolutely prohibits (Romans 3:23–27; 4:2–6; 9:31–32; 11:5–6; Galatians 2:16; 3:2–5, 10; Ephesians 2:8–9; Second Timothy 1:9; Titus 3:5; please read these in your own Bible). If salvation is not totally, completely God's work, or if we have participated in the salvation decision, it is not real salvation, as we and our work (efforts) are totally unacceptable to God. Think what could happen if we were involved with our own salvation. We are not the smartest beings in the universe, compared to God's perfection. We would do something stupid, like accidentally drop our salvation and lose it. Or do something incredibly stupid, like get tired of carrying our salvation around with us and drop it off someplace! Thank God that His plan of salvation is salvation by grace alone, accepted on our part, by faith, which He gave at the end of His work of grace for salvation. Romans 8:28–39 directly address the perfection of His plan.

At this point, the question must be asked of ourselves, "Am I truly saved?" Did I, without great urging in my spirit that I was not worthy of being one of God's children, make the decision that I would be saved, and say the words, or thought the thoughts, of salvation, just because I thought it would be nice? Make sure of your salvation if there is any doubt. Was it really God's work?

FAITH

Regarding salvation, when we look at Ephesians 2:8–9, we see that, along with grace, faith is mentioned: "For by grace you have been saved through faith. And this is not your own doing; it is the gift of God, not a result of works, so that no one may boast." Faith, along with grace, is a gift from God. The last phrases of the passage are, "that not of yourselves: it is the gift of God: Not of works, lest any man should boast." God does not want salvation to involve our effort, our work(s). If salvation did involve our efforts, it would be compromised and could be used wrongly, or even given up. But since it is only God's effort, or work, salvation is perfect, even though we are not perfect. Our salvation is in His powerful, righteous right hand and cannot be affected in any way for any of those who are saved!

Where does faith come from? We have faith since birth. Babies have faith that they will be fed and loved. They have faith that their father or other loved one will not drop them. As the babies grow older into childhood, they have faith that nighttime will come and daytime will follow. As they grow older, they have faith that they will not fall off the edge of the world. As they continue to grow, they have faith that when they want to sit down or lie down, their chair, sofa, or bed will not move or break as they are in the process of sitting or lying down. The Gospels teach us, after Jesus miraculously fed them and healed many, that He was the Messiah who was prophesied to lead the nation into independence by forcibly taking the yoke of Rome from their nation (John 6:14–15). He did not do that on His first coming. Because He did not do what they wanted, they believed that when Jesus was arrested, beaten, and crucified, that Rome acted properly. The Bible tells us that many Jews believed (John 8:30; 10:42). Most of these "believing" Jews lost their "belief" when Jesus revealed more of who He was (John 6:60, 64–65; 12:37–38). They rejected the "suffering servant" but greatly desired the King, who is yet to come. These Jews who fell away had false faith; they had faith in what they wanted to be true instead of what was actually true. Faith is not true faith unless it "Now faith is the assurance of things hoped for, the conviction of things not seen" (Hebrews 11:1). Because most faith is, like freewill, corrupted by self-centeredness, it cannot believe in Jesus Christ as Savior. Saving faith must be from God.

Ephesians 2:8–9 tells us that faith, along with grace, is a gift from God, not generated within ourselves, so that no person can boast that it is *my* faith that saved me! The Bible says, over and over, that faith comes from God or from Jesus Christ, who is God. We see the phrase, "faith of" Jesus Christ, God, etc., several times in the KJV (you won't find this interpretation in most other versions, but I believe the KJV is correct):

- Romans 3:3 (emphasis added) states, "What if some were unfaithful? Does their faithlessness nullify the *faithfulness of God*?"

- Galatians 2:16 (emphasis added) states, "Knowing that a man is not justified by the works of the law, but by the *faith of Jesus Christ*, even we have believed in Jesus Christ, that we might be justified by the *faith of Christ*, and not by the works of the law: for by the works of the law shall no flesh be justified" (KJV). John Gill, an old time Baptist preacher, stated in John Gill's Expositor, in his notes on Galatians 2:16 (Online Bible Edition, Version 5.10.00.03, June 25, 2016, Copyright 1992-2016) "'but by the faith of Jesus Christ'; not by that faith, which Christ, as man, had in God, who promised him help, succor, and assistance, and for which he, as man, trusted in him, and exercised faith upon him; but that faith of which he (Christ) is the object, author, and finisher; and not by that as a cause, for faith has no causal influence on the justification (salvation) of a sinner; it is not the efficient cause, for it is God that justifies; nor the moving cause, or which induces (encourages) God to justify any, for that is his own free grace and good will." In other words, saving faith is not of the saved person, but is from Jesus Christ. There is nothing that a person can do to form faith in Christ until after the moment of salvation, after which the gift of faith from Christ becomes the faith in Christ.

CHRISTIAN LIFE GOD'S WAY

- Galatians 2:20 (emphasis added) states, "I am crucified with Christ: nevertheless I live; yet not I, but Christ liveth in me: and the life which I now live in the flesh I live by the *faith of the Son of God*, who loved me, and gave himself for me" (KJV).

- Philippians 3:9 (emphasis added) states, "And be found in him, not having mine own righteousness, which is of the law, but that which is through the *faith of Christ*, the *righteousness which is of God by faith*" (KJV)

We see that faith, along with grace, is "not your own doing, it is the *gift* of God" (Ephesians. 2:8). Many Christians believe that faith is generated from within themselves, from nothing, or from a memory of God that is in all human beings. No, Biblical faith did not generate itself within ourselves when we heard the Gospel. Where, then, does faith come from. Let's follow a biblical thread to determine where faith comes from.

> Now we know that whatever the law says it speaks to those who are under the law, so that every mouth may be stopped, and the whole world may be held accountable to God. For by works of the law no human being will be justified in his sight, since through the law comes knowledge of sin. But now the righteousness of God has been manifested apart from the law, although the Law and the Prophets bear witness to it—the righteousness of God through faith in Jesus Christ for all who believe. For there is no distinction: (Romans 3:19–22)

This is quite a mouthful, but it can be easily understood if we break it down (expose the passage through an exposition).

- Everything that the Law states pertains to everyone that is under the Law.

- No one can claim any excuse because every mouth will be stopped; it is understood that everyone is under the Law and has no excuse.

37

- Because everyone is under the Law, everyone is guilty before God.

- By the deeds of the Law (anything done without the Righteousness of God) no one can be justified (made right with God).

- Now, with the suffering, death and resurrection of Jesus Christ, there is a new form of righteousness, which never existed before, that is now made known. It is the righteousness without the Law, or outside of the Law, although it was promised in the OT Law and the prophets!

- This new righteousness is not an addition to the character of God. Instead, it is a newly manifested form of His righteousness that He imputes to those who believe in the atoning work of His Son.

- That new righteousness of God the Father, through Jesus Christ, the Only Begotten Son of God, is given to all who believe (the belief must include trust via the faith that is from God). It is not actual righteousness. It is imputed righteousness that makes a believer acceptable before God the Father, even though the person is not actually righteous; He or she is forgiven through the perfect life of the Only Begotten Son, His perfect sacrificial atonement, and His being risen from the dead, making this new righteousness possible.

- There is no difference between Jew and Gentile regarding the new righteousness.

A verse that easily follows Romans 3:19–22, regarding the question "where does faith come from?" is Romans 1:17: "For in it the righteousness of God is revealed from faith for faith, as it is written, 'The righteous shall live by faith.'" This, like the previous passage, is not easy to understand but is another buried treasure that is so great that the finder sells his physical possessions like he can buy the field in which he found the buried treasure, the pearl of great price which the finder sells his physical possessions so that he can buy the pearl

(Matthew 13:44–46). Let's look at Romans 1:17, like we did with the previous passage, to find what God is telling us with this verse.

- The phrase "therein is the righteousness of God revealed" is the same imputed righteousness of Jesus Christ that we found in Romans 3:21–22. It makes a believer acceptable to God the Father, even though the person is not actually righteous.

- That righteousness is "revealed from faith for faith." This is a seemingly difficult phrase, "faith for faith." There are almost as many interpretations of what it means as there are commentary writers who are brave enough to comment on it. I don't think there is a reason to question what it means; it is pretty clear if you let God interpret the phrase for you, which He did in Romans 3:22: "the righteousness of God through faith in Jesus Christ for all who believe. For there is no distinction:" The first faith is the faith that the Father had in Jesus Christ, who made the new, imputed righteousness possible. When grace has done its work, and the person is becoming a believer, that faith of God the Father in Jesus Christ is given, just like grace, to the new believer (John Gill's Expositor and Vincent's NT Word Studies, for this verse in the *Open Bible* computer program).

- God, through Paul, states, "as it is written, 'The righteous shall live by faith.'" This is a quote from Habakkuk 2:4b (emphasis added): "But the just shall live *by his faith*."

Philippians 3:9 states, "and be found in him, not having a righteousness of my own that comes from the law, but that which comes through faith in Christ, the righteousness from God that depends on faith—"

We see, from Ephesians 2:8–9, that grace and faith are both essential to salvation. Grace and faith are both free gifts from God. We are not actively involved in either grace or faith, to the point of salvation. Grace is not rejected, making faith possible. God is the active party. When a person receives that faith, he or she can now accept what has already been done, by the grace of God. The new believer can verify the salvation that God's grace has already given us.

Once grace has softened our self-centered freewill to the point of yielding, God gives us faith so that, by that faith, we can accept the salvation of God, which has already happened in our heart, from God. Then we can verbally affirm that we are saved: Romans 10:9–10 states, "because, if you confess with your mouth that Jesus is Lord and believe in your heart that God raised him from the dead, you will be saved. For with the heart one believes and is justified, and with the mouth one confesses and is saved."

A Person's free will, since the fall, is very powerfully self-centered. For salvation to occur, grace must neutralize free will. How does that occur or not occur?

For a person who has not accepted Jesus Christ as his or her Savior, God wants that person to be saved. Grace is God's love, the Word of God, and the Holy Spirit all working as a team. God showers that person with grace.

1.   For the person who will be saved, the person experiences a conviction of sin, knowledge that a Savior is required, and a peaceful attraction to the person of God through Jesus Christ and His love. As grace works, the person is turned by God towards Him. The person does not rely upon free will. As the person is, by grace, drawn towards God, God gives the person faith to believe. This is all passive to the person, but totally active as God's work, leading to the active action to accept Jesus Christ as Savior by God's power of grace.

2.   For the person who will not be saved, the person experiences a peaceful, truthful, holy attraction. This attraction goes contrary to what the person wants to experience. Instead of passively letting grace neutralize his or her free will, the person activates his or her free will, thus effectively neutralizing grace. This is all the work of the person to deny the grace of God.

3

SATAN'S FALL

It is very common for us to hear and believe that Satan fell before the creation of mankind, or even before the creation of things living on earth. We have grown up with the theory of evolution. We have toyed with theistic evolution. Many Christian colleges even teach the *Big Bang* theory with millions and billions of years as the biblical model of creation.

We also have many Christians and scholars supporting the *gap* theory, which teaches that there is a great gap between the first day of creation and the second. During this *gap*, there was supposedly some kind of civilization, with or without people, that existed. Satan fell, and God destroyed creation so that He could recreate. That is why, this theory teaches, the earth was "without form and void." Many of the conservative commentaries and books on theology, going back seventy five to over one hundred years ago, referred to the gap theory. They were, of course, wrong in this area.

In these theories, we kind of lose sight of who Satan is and why he rebelled against God. There are plenty of ideas about when and why Satan fell. But have we ever really studied the Bible to see what God says about Satan's fall? We may find something quite interesting about Satan and about how he sees mankind.

Part of Ezekiel 28 is commonly accepted as a description of *Satan*. God condemns the Ammonites, the Moabites, the Edomites and the Philistines in Ezekiel 25. Then, in chapters 26–27, God goes on to the city of *Tyre*, a very rich and powerful city-state. Then, in Ezekiel 28, God condemns the king of Tyre. We can see, by the passage that the king of Tyre was a *type* of Satan. Then in chapter 28, verses 11–16, God turns the passage from a human king to Satan, himself. The passage is still applied to the king of Tyre in a figurative way, but it definitely fits Satan. We can see the transition to a supernatural being because no physical person could have filled the description given. Only Satan could fill this description.

Let's read Ezekiel 28:11–16:

> Moreover, the word of the LORD came to me: "Son of man, raise a lamentation over the king of Tyre, and say to him, Thus says the Lord GOD: "You were the signet of perfection, full of wisdom and perfect in beauty. You were in Eden, the garden of God; every precious stone was your covering, sardius, topaz, and diamond, beryl, onyx, and jasper, sapphire, emerald, and carbuncle; and crafted in gold were your settings and your engravings. On the day that you were created they were prepared. You were an anointed guardian cherub. I placed you; you were on the holy mountain of God; in the midst of the stones of fire you walked. You were blameless in your ways from the day you were created, till unrighteousness was found in you. In the abundance of your trade you were filled with violence in your midst, and you sinned; so I cast you as a profane thing from the mountain of God, and I destroyed you, O guardian cherub, from the midst of the stones of fire.

Another passage commonly accepted as being about Satan is in Isaiah 14, which starts with a prophesy about Israel. God will, after the Great Tribulation, give the Jews rest from their sorrow, and from their fear, and from the hard bondage wherein they were made to serve. Then, Isaiah starts a prophesy about the king of Babylon.

This was written before Babylon became the great power that overcame and destroyed Jerusalem. Assyria was the great power at this time, and Egypt was a second- rate power. Babylon was still a rather young, developing power. But God prophesied that the king of Babylon was a wicked oppressor who would come against Jerusalem, the Golden City, and destroy it. This passage also has meaning about the Antichrist in the Great Tribulation. Then God says that He will destroy "the staff of the wicked, the scepter of rulers" (Isaiah 14:5).

Next comes a prophesy of the millennium kingdom that also refers to the near future king of Babylon, the king that brought Judah out of Jerusalem and into captivity, and, at the same time, the future Antichrist, "All of them will answer and say to you: 'You too have become as weak as we! You have become like us!' Your pomp is brought down to Sheol, the sound of your harps; maggots are laid as a bed beneath you, and worms are your covers (Isaiah 14:10–11).

The king of Babylon is, in this passage, like the king of Tyre in Ezekiel, a *type* of Satan. In Isaiah 14:12–15, we see the passage has transitioned, in a figurative sense, from the king of Babylon, to Satan.

> How you are fallen from heaven, *O Day Star* [Lucifer], son of Dawn! How you are cut down to the ground, you who laid the nations low! You said in your heart, 'I will ascend to heaven; above the stars of God I will set my throne on high; I will sit on the mount of assembly in the far reaches of the north; I will ascend above the heights of the clouds; I will make myself like the *Most High*.' But you are brought down to Sheol, to the far reaches of the pit. (Isaiah 14:12–15; emphasis added)

Then the passage goes back to the king of Babylon. *Lucifer*, according to Jewish tradition, is the name Satan had before his fall (Lewis Sperry Chafer, Systematic Theology, Kregel Publications, Kregel, Inc., Grand rapids, MI 49501, 1976, vol. 1, pg 239, vol. 2, pg. 246).

Between these two passages, we can learn a lot about Lucifer, who became Satan, and the first sin. Look at the description that God, through Ezekiel, gave Lucifer, before he fell into sin, in Ezekiel 28:12b: "You were the signet of perfection, full of wisdom and perfect in beauty." God stated, through Ezekiel, that Lucifer was sealed as being perfect. In other words, he was the perfection of perfectness, including in his appearance. There was nothing missing in Lucifer. Everything about Lucifer pointed to the perfection of God.

The cherub is the angel that is always *praising* God. Look at Lucifer's description: Ezekiel 28:13 states "every precious stone was your covering, sardius, topaz, and diamond, beryl, onyx, and jasper, sapphire, emerald, and carbuncle; and crafted in gold." Similar descriptions of the precious stones and gold was used in two other places in the Bible. They were on the *breastplate* of the high priest of the Old Testament worship, and they were in the description of the foundation of the city walls around *New Jerusalem* in Revelation 21.

The next descriptions of Lucifer's makeup are different in newer Bible versions from the older versions. The newer versions, in Ezekiel 28:13, state similar language to the ESV: "were your *settings* and your *engravings*." The older versions say something like the KJV, "the workmanship of thy *tabrets* and of thy *pipes* was prepared in thee in the day that thou wast created."

The *tabret* (Strong's 08596) was a *percussion* instrument, a timbrel or tamborine. The Hebrew word means "to beat." It made music by shaking or *beating* it. If you read the commentaries, the older commentaries all interpret the last part of verse 13 the same way the KJV, NAS, and NKJ do. The newer commentaries either don't mention it, or go with the newer English versions. The exact Hebrew word is used also in Genesis 31:27; Exodus 15:20; Judges 11:34; 1 Samuel 10:5, 18:6; 2 Samuel 6:5; 1 Chronicles 13:8; Job 21:12; Psalm 81:2, 149:3, 150:4; Isaiah 5:12, 24:8, 30:32; and Jeremiah 31:4. In every one of these other passages, the word is translated as a timbrel, tambourine, or similar instrument; and this is true with every one of the translations that did not interpret the Hebrew word as a musical instrument in Exekiel 28:13. Why do most of the modern versions have an aversion to having Satan's makeup include musical instruments? Could it be the same reason that made rock music acceptable to the Church—compromise with the world?

The Hebrew word translated "pipes" is Strong's 05345. It means, literally, a *hole*, or a hole *bored through*. It can sort of be forced to mean a jeweler's mount for precious stones, which can fit the verse, and is used in some of the newer translations. Why would the word translated 'pipes' be separated from the precious stones in the text, by a musical instrument (the words are in the same order in the English as they are in the Hebrew)? The word can also mean a *pipe*, which is simply a hole covered by matter, or a hole bored through a stick or piece of wood. It especially can mean a pipe with holes drilled in it, a *flute-type* instrument. It is a musical *wind* instrument.

The King James version has the correct interpretation of the passage; the meanings of the words *tabrets* and *pipes* are musical instruments, meant for praise to God. It is the old understanding and fits the context of the Bible as a whole.

Satan was made with precious stones that, in two other places in the Bible, are symbolic of belonging to God: in the high priest's bib, and in New Jerusalem. He is also made up of *musical instruments* so he could continuously praise God with music. What is obvious is that Satan used music against God, against God's people, and to keep captive his own people (all who are not God's people). Rock music is just a continuance of Satan's attack. The lyrics may be meant to honor God, nature or idols; the musical score absolutely honors Satan. Who do you want to honor with your music?

Note that musical instruments were part of Satan's makeup. God intended music to be part of worship of Him right from the beginning of time. Part of the task of the cherubim was to worship God. Satan was created to use musical instruments in his praise of God. We Christians use musical instruments to worship God. What happened to some of the music when Satan fell? He took music with him. We have good music, as originally created by God; and we have bad music, started when Satan fell into sin. This is not about the lyrics in music; it is about the musical score itself. There is moral value in the type of music we listen to, in spite of what most Contemporary Christian Music fans want to believe. Music has, for many generations, been called the universal language as it affects the psyche so much. Instrumental music will either praise to God Almighty, or it will praise Satan. Who do you want to praise?

Satan was created as a *cherub*, the *head* of all the cherubs. In Ezekiel 28:14, God calls Satan "an anointed guardian cherub. I placed you." The KJV does not use the word *an*, but *the* the anointed cherub, which fits the context. A literal interpretation for "I have placed you" is "and I have put you in the height of Holy God where he walked up and down in magnificence." Satan was most likely the *chief cherub*. In general, it appears that Lucifer was the most beautiful and powerful being ever created. Lewis Sperry Chafer, in his Systematic Theology, states, in at least two places, that Satan (Lucifer) was the highest of the angels (Ibid. vol. 1, pg 239; vol. 2, pg. 246). He was "the anointed cherub that covereth" (KJV). The ESV calls him the "anointed guardian cherub."

The word "Anointed" (Strong's #4473), is found only in Ezekiel 28:14. A form of the word means "expanse," such as "wings expanded," but that is not the word Ezekiel used. The word, when used in a religious sense, actually seems to mean "to anoint," such as the act of anointing with oil, and even the Anointed One, the Messiah (Theological Wordbook of the Old Testament (TWOT), Moody Bible Institute of Chicago, 1980, #1255d).

Satan (Lucifer before he rebelled against God) had been the chief of the cherubim. He was the chief cherub. Satan had been a God-praising cherub with wings outstretched, covering God, a position of preeminence, and probably in a symbolic position of guardian and protector of God's presence. He had been created to be awesomely beautiful (verse 12), a praise to God. He had musical instruments built into him, also to praise God in music. He had been the created being that was closest to God. Jesus Christ was his direct authority, or supervisor. They knew each other very well, and since God has always been perfect and Satan had been perfect before he rebelled, they worked very well together.

Ezekiel 28:14 says that Satan was "on the holy mountain of God." Satan had therefore been in God's presence because the "holy mountain" was the seat of God's authority. Then, in verse 16, we see that Satan "wast perfect in thy ways from the day that thou wast created, till iniquity was found in thee" [KJV]. He sinned by rebelling against God.

From Ezekiel 28, let's go to Isaiah 14:12–14:

> How you are fallen from heaven, O Day Star, son of
> Dawn! How you are cut down to the ground, you who
> laid the nations low! You said in your heart, 'I will ascend
> to heaven; above the stars of God I will set my throne
> on high; I will sit on the mount of assembly in the far
> reaches of the north; I will ascend above the heights of
> the clouds; I will make myself like the Most High.'

Before his fall into iniquity, Satan was the most important of all the created beings, except for mankind. He had a position of authority greater than that of any other created being. He had it all! Something happened to make him want more. What could that have been? Note the phrase in Isaiah 14:13, "I will sit also upon the mount of the congregation." The word *congregation* here means "appointed place of meeting." The mount of the congregation is the place appointed for God to meet with God's crown of creation, people (Psalm 2:6; Psalm 121:1; Isaiah 8:18; Micah 4:2).

Go back to Ezekiel 28:13: "You were in Eden, the garden of God." Something very special happened in Eden. Look at Genesis 3:8a, "And they (Adam and Eve) heard the sound of the LORD God walking in the garden in the cool of the day." Eden was the first place where God came, in person, as Jesus Christ, to meet with mankind (Why Jesus Christ? God the Father and God the Holy Spirit are Spirits; the Bible never has them take the form of a person. There are several instances of Jesus Christ making pre-incarnation appearances, or Theophanies, on Earth to mankind.) Eden, before sin occurred, was figuratively the "mountain of God," where God walked and talked with mankind, Adam and Eve, in the cool the day, and where God was worshiped. Satan was with God, Jesus Christ, in his position of honor guard, guarding the second person of the Trinity when He met with Adam and Eve in the garden of Eden.

Up to this point, where Satan accompanied Jesus Christ into the garden of Eden, what was there in God's creation that would have tempted Satan to rebel against God, tempted to usurp God's power and authority? According to Isaiah 14, Satan wanted to be in the place of God, or even higher than God. Satan wanted to be more important than God. What caused Satan to sin? Remember, Satan was not only the chief cherub, he was the cherub that covers, or guards, the holiness of God. He was with God. He accompanied Jesus Christ when God walked and talked with Adam and Eve. If anything threatened to violate the holiness of God, Satan had the power and authority to destroy it. His position was a position of power and honor. He was next to God. He was in the garden of Eden, with Jesus Christ, as a perfect being. But he rebelled against God. Look back at Ezekiel 28:15: "You were blameless in your ways from the day you were created, till unrighteousness was found in you."

Let's look further at what the *cherub* is in the Bible. In the Tabernacle, golden cherubim were placed, wings outstretched, over the *mercy seat* of the ark of the covenant. Exodus 25:22 (emphasis added) states, "There I will meet with you, and from above the mercy seat, from between the two cherubim that are on the ark of the testimony, I will *speak* with you about all that I will give you in commandment for the people of Israel." God met with *mankind* to communicate with mankind between the cherubim.

Examples of God's meeting mankind between the cherubim

1. When Moses and the people of Israel completed setting up and dedicating the Tabernacle, Moses went into the Tabernacle to talk to God. Numbers 7:89 (emphasis added) states, "And when Moses was gone into the tabernacle of the congregation to speak with him (God), then he heard the voice of one (God) speaking unto him from off the mercy seat that was upon the ark of testimony, from between the two cherubims: and he (God) spake unto him (Moses)."

2. The high priest went into the holy of holies, once a year, to *present* the people before the Lord. Hebrews 9:1–7 states, "Now even the first covenant had regulations for worship and an earthly place of holiness. For a tent [Tabernacle] was prepared, the first section, in which were the lampstand and the table and the bread of the Presence. It is

called the Holy Place. Behind the second curtain was a second section called the Most Holy Place, having the golden altar of incense and the ark of the covenant covered on all sides with gold, in which was a golden urn holding the manna, and Aaron's staff that budded, and the tablets of the covenant. Above it were the cherubim of glory overshadowing the mercy seat. Of these things we cannot now speak in detail. These preparations having thus been made, the priests go regularly into the first section, performing their ritual duties, but into the second only the high priest goes, and he but once a year, and not without taking blood, which he offers for himself and for the unintentional sins of the people.

The Mercy Seat, the lid of the Ark of the covenant, over which the two golden cherubim had their wings outstretched, was where God met with the representative of His chosen people to accept the sacrifice made in intercession for the people to God. The Mercy Seat, over which the golden cherubim had their wings outstretched, was the place where God met with mankind.

What were the cherubim? What did they do? Here is a list of six things the cherubim do.

- The chief duty of the cherub was to be a protector, focused on the Person and the *holiness* of God. Lewis Sperry Chafer, founder of Dallas Theological Institute, states, in his Systematic Theology, vol. 2, pg. 42, "This group of angels [cherubim] is related to the throne of God as protectors and defenders of His holiness." He quotes Ezekiel. 28:14, where God states that Lucifer, before he fell, was "on the holy mountain of God." He also gives several other references, pointing to Mountain of God, that, in the Old Testament, is the seat of God's authority (Exodus 4:27; Psalm 2:6, 3:4, 43:3, 68:15; Isaiah 2:2, 11:9). The cherubim were protectors of God's holiness, even at the throne of God. The question arises, does God need a protector of *Himself* or His holiness? No, of course, He doesn't. But this is what God has chosen to reveal about Himself, that He is so important that He deserves very large honor guard. He has the cherubim around Himself always, and the cherubim are protectors, even if just symbolic in nature. They bring attention to the holiness and glory of God.

- When Adam and Eve had sinned, God sent them out of the garden of Eden. To prevent them, or any future person, from ever entering, God "drove out the man; and he placed at the east of the garden of Eden Cherubim and a flaming sword which turned every way, to keep the way of the tree of life (Genesis 3:24). The cherubim were guardians.

- The cherubim were, as mentioned before, over the mercy seat of the ark of the covenant:

Exodus 25:18–22 states, "And you shall make two cherubim of gold; of hammered work shall you make them, on the two ends of the mercy seat. Make one cherub on the one end, and one cherub on the other end. Of one piece with the mercy seat shall you make the cherubim on its two ends. The cherubim shall spread out their wings above, overshadowing the mercy seat with their wings, their faces one to another; toward the mercy seat shall the faces of the cherubim be. And you shall put the mercy seat on the top of the ark, and in the ark you shall put the testimony that I shall give you. There I will meet with you, and from above the mercy seat, from between the two cherubim that are on the ark of the testimony, I will speak with you about all that I will give you in commandment for the people of Israel." The Mercy Seat of the Arc of the Covenant, with the cherubs covering the seat, was a meeting place between God and mankind. God figuratively sat on His Mercy Seat, accepting the blood sacrifice of the Old Testament chosen people and having mercy on them. The Mercy Seat was guarded by the cherubim. The blood of the Old Testament sacrifice pointed to the shed blood of Jesus Christ, which was once and for all (Hebrews 10:10).

- The veil, or curtain, in the Tabernacle, between the Holy place and the Holy of Holies, had cherubim sewed into the fabric (Exodus 26:1, 31).

- When Solomon had the Temple built, there were two golden cherubim inside the Holy of Holies, each with wings outstretched. One wing touched one wall inside the Holy of Holies, while the other touched the wing of the other cherubim, which was the same size. Each cherubim was fifteen to eighteen feet tall with outstretched wings fifteen to eighteen feet from wingtip to wingtip, approximately thirty to thirty six feet across. They, together, stretched across the width of the Temple. The Ark of the Covenant was placed underneath those cherubim (1 Kings 6 and 8).

- In Solomon's temple, cherubim, as well as lions, palm trees, flowers, etc., were carved into the walls (1 Kings 6 and 7).

This means there was one huge pair of golden cherubim in the Holy of Holies, one smaller pair, over the mercy seat, cherubim woven into the curtain veil, and cherubim carved into the walls of the temple. Cherubim were important in the meeting place between God and mankind. God was said to dwell between the cherubim. Second Kings 19:15 states, "And Hezekiah prayed before the LORD and said: "O LORD the God of Israel, who is enthroned above the cherubim, you are the God, you alone, of all the kingdoms of the earth; you have made heaven and earth."

- Ezekiel 1 gives us that famous vision of four beings supporting and transporting the throne of God. In chapter 10, those beings are identified as cherubim. In chapter 9, God was telling how Jerusalem was going to be punished for its idolatry. The cherubim were present, and God must have been present. In chapter 10, the Cherubim were present when the *Shekinah* Glory (Glorious Presence) of God left the Temple and went over the Cherubim. In Ezekiel 10:5, we are told, "And the sound of the wings of the cherubim was heard as far as the outer court, like the voice of God Almighty when he speaks." God left His place of ministering to His chosen people.

- In Ezekiel 28:13, Satan, the chief cherub who covers, had, in his makeup, beautiful stones and musical instruments. The beauty and musical instruments were to praise, worship, and honor God.

- In Ezekiel 41, when Ezekiel was given the vision of the future Temple, cherubim were again carved into the walls and furniture.

What do these passages and other similar passages tell us about cherubim and Satan, as he was created?

- They indicated the presence of God.

- They were "honor" guardians of the holiness of God.

- They apparently accompanied God in God's missions.

- They did work for God.

- They praised God with musical instruments and beauty.

Now we can join the two main portions of Scripture that reveal Satan to us, Ezekiel 28:11–16 and Isaiah 14:11–15.

God, through Isaiah, told us that Satan stated, "I will sit on the mount of assembly" (Isaiah 14:13). This means that Satan wanted to sit at the appointed place of meeting which, in the beginning, was in the Garden of Eden, where God walked and talked with Adam and Eve. Why did Satan want to usurp God's place there? Satan saw these human beings who, unlike any other part of creation, were given the ability to choose to obey or disobey their Creator. This was obvious to Satan, because God, Jesus Christ, accompanied by His honor guard, Lucifer, had told Adam, "And the LORD God commanded the man, saying, 'You may surely eat of every tree of the garden, but of the tree of the knowledge of good and evil you shall not eat, for in the day that you eat of it you shall surely die'" (Genesis 2:16–17). *Never, before Satan saw Adam and Eve, did Satan see a being who was given the freewill choice to worship God or not worship Him.* Satan was already the most exalted of all the angels (Ezekiel 28:14). He was already perfect ("You were the signet of perfection, full of wisdom and perfect in beauty." [Ezekiel 28:12b]). Satan was not led astray by wanting to be worshiped by angels; he was already the chief of the angels that were the closest to God. But other than angels, only Adam and Eve (people) were given the choice to obey and worship God. In fact, the opportunity to disobey God was placed right before them (the tree of the knowledge of good and evil). To have someone worship him because they wanted to, of their own freewill, was something that Satan did not have. Satan decided that he wanted to be in control and wanted to be worshiped by these beings whom God had given the freedom to choose to do right or wrong, to honor God or themselves.

APPLICATION

Satan did not fall before Creation was complete, as we may have heard in the past. It is very crucial to understand why Satan fell. Satan did not just begin to desire to take God's place of preeminence. Satan sinned because we, mankind, were created to worship God and have a relationship with Him and have the choice whether or not to do so. Satan wanted to be worshiped by someone who had the choice to do so. Satan wanted and still does want us to worship him.

Why is this so important? What is the difference if Satan rebelled against God before creation was completed, before He created the crown of His creation (people) who He wants to have a relationship with, or after?

Satan is the enemy of all mankind, not because of any part of creation before mankind was created but because of mankind. He wants our worship. He wants us to choose him, not God. Satan, who was Lucifer, very quickly gained part of what he wanted. Satan does not attack the people who he already possesses, but he has declared war on all whom have, by grace, believed in that Perfect Sacrifice, and who have gained eternal life.

Satan is our enemy if we have become Christians, because Satan doesn't want our worship of God to be effective. He cannot make us lose our salvation, in spite of what many want to believe. Therefore, he tries to destroy our testimonies. His very rebellion was directed toward the goal of getting mankind to worship him. Because he can't do that with believers, he does everything he can to keep us from worshiping God or being useful to God. If we will not worship him, he does not want us to worship God either. Nothing else is important to him. He has declared war on Christians and that war is, to Satan, an "anything goes" war, limited only by God Almighty.

CONCLUSION

Let's look at this from our point of view, where we are. We human beings are the reason for Satan's rebellion. Nothing else was important enough for Satan to turn against God. What does that say about us? We, people created in the image of God, are the crowning glory of His creation. We were created to worship Him, to have the personal experience of a wonderful relationship with Him. Nothing else in creation is so important to God as us, each member of mankind. Jesus Christ, God Himself, the Second Person of the Trinity, became man, never ceasing to be God, but having humanity forever added to His being God. In His humanity (His incarnation), He suffered, shed blood, and died for us (Philippians 2:5–11). We are important to God. He loves us. He offers us something that Satan could never have offered, which is a personal relationship with Him that surpasses even His relationship to angels. He also has complete control over Satan; He allows Satan only the power that He chooses to permit, which, admittedly, is too much power for us to face. Not even Michael, the archangel, would try to stand up against Satan. Jude 1:9 states, "But when the archangel Michael, contending with the devil, was disputing about the body of Moses, he did not presume to pronounce a blasphemous judgment, but said, 'The Lord rebuke you.'" Our God has no reason to be afraid of Satan. With Him, all things, according to His plan, are possible.

- Mark 10:27 states, "Jesus looked at them and said, 'With man it is impossible, but not with God. For all things are possible with God.'" This takes faith and trust. God will never tempt us, but He will, when He decides that it is best, let us be tempted. He knows that, through the temptation, we will learn to let Him be Lord and learn to trust Him more. Yes, with God, Satan can be defeated.

- First Corinthians 10:13 states, "No temptation has overtaken you that is not common to man. God is faithful, and he will not let you be tempted beyond your ability, but with the temptation he will also provide the way of escape, that you may be able to endure it."

There have been different theories about when Satan rebelled against God with Adam and Eve. There is something missing in every other reason given for Satan's fall than what is portrayed in this study, as he had everything, everything except the worship of created beings that had a choice, mankind, the last part of God's creation and the crown of His creation. To this day, there are still only two lords, God through Jesus Christ, or Satan:

- Romans 6:16 states, "Do you not know that if you present yourselves to anyone as obedient slaves, you are slaves of the one whom you obey, either of sin, which leads to death, or of obedience, which leads to righteousness?"

- Matthew 6:24 states, "No one can serve two masters, for either he will hate the one and love the other, or he will be devoted to the one and despise the other. You cannot serve God and money."

4

COMPROMISE

A STUDY OF 1 CORINTHIANS 8–10

The church at Corinth had problems. They split into groups of followers of different pastors or teachers rather than following Jesus Christ. They *lovingly* looked the other way when the serious sin of a kind that did not occur even among pagans (First Corinthians 5:1). They took each other to civil court. They participated in idol worship. And they did many more things that Paul called them to repentance about. The letter the Corinthians wrote to Paul had, in part, something to say about food that had been offered to idols. The first letter of Paul written to the Corinthians, chapters 8-10, had Paul's response to this part of their letter.

Let's look specifically at the participation in idol worship given us in First Corinthians 8.

> Now concerning food offered to idols: "we know that
> all of us possess knowledge." This "knowledge" puffs up,
> but love builds up. If anyone imagines that he knows

something, he does not yet know as he ought to know. But if anyone loves God, he is known by God. Therefore, as to the eating of food offered to idols, we know that "an idol has no real existence," and that "there is no God but one." For although there may be so-called gods in heaven or on earth—as indeed there are many "gods" and many "lords"— yet for us there is one God, the Father, from whom are all things and for whom we exist, and one Lord, Jesus Christ, through whom are all things and through whom we exist. However, not all possess this knowledge. But some, through former association with idols, eat food as really offered to an idol, and their conscience, being weak, is defiled. Food will not commend us to God. We are no worse off if we do not eat, and no better off if we do. But take care that this right of yours does not somehow become a stumbling block to the weak. For if anyone sees you who have knowledge eating in an idol's temple, will he not be encouraged, if his conscience is weak, to eat food offered to idols? And so by your knowledge this weak person is destroyed, the brother for whom Christ died. Thus, sinning against your brothers and wounding their conscience when it is weak, you sin against Christ. Therefore, if food makes my brother stumble, I will never eat meat, lest I make my brother stumble (First Corinthians 8:1–13).

Paul starts his letter with the introduction statement given in First Corinthians 8:1a, "Now concerning food offered to idols:"

Paul quotes or summarizes the Corinthians in First Corinthians 8:1a, "'we know that all of us possess knowledge.'"

Paul responds, "This 'knowledge' puffs up, but love (*agape*) builds up. If anyone imagines that he knows something, he does not yet know as he ought to know" (your knowledge is not adequate).

The Corinthians letter had written in First Corinthians 8:3-6, "But if anyone loves God, he is known by God. Therefore, as to the eating of food offered to idols, we know that 'an idol has no real existence,' and that 'there is no God but one.' For although there may be so-called gods in heaven or on earth—as indeed there are many 'gods' and many 'lords'—yet for us there is one God, the Father, from whom are all things and for whom we exist, and one Lord, Jesus Christ, through whom are all things and through whom we exist." They stated that there is only one God and the idols are nothing. Because of that, food offered to the idols is offered to nothing. Therefore, there is no danger or sin.

The Corinthians letter, continued in verses 7-8: "However, not all possess this knowledge. But some, through former association with idols, eat food as really offered to an idol, and their conscience, being weak, is defiled. Food will not commend us to God. We are no worse off if we do not eat, and no better off if we do." They complained that, in spite of the fact that they believed food had no intrinsic value. there were those of weak faith who did not agree with them.

Paul responded to this last complaint in verses 9-13, "But take care that this right of yours does not somehow become a stumbling block to the weak. For if anyone sees you who have knowledge eating in an idol's temple, will he not be encouraged, if his conscience is weak, to eat food offered to idols? And so by your knowledge this weak person is destroyed, the brother for whom Christ died. Thus, sinning against your brothers and wounding their conscience when it is weak, you sin against Christ. Therefore, if food makes my brother stumble, I will never eat meat, lest I make my brother stumble." Paul told them that their liberty brought on by the puffed up knowledge (v. 1) made them suffer loss of *agape* love, because there are some who believe that the meat is offered to idols.

You may have noted that Paul did not address the first part of the Corinthian argument given in First Corinthians 8:4-8. That part of the letter was so important that He wanted to wait until he had addressed the easier part given in First Corinthians 8 so that he could get into just what the ramifications were of what the Corinthians had written about regarding to food offered to idols.

In chapter 9, Paul teaches that, as teachers of the gospel of Jesus Christ, they should not have had physical needs. Those who are taught should pay for the living of those who teach. First Corinthians 9:13–14 states, "Do you not know that those who minister the holy things eat of the things of the temple, and those who serve at the altar partake of the offerings of the altar? Even so the Lord has commanded that those who preach the gospel should live from the gospel." This is doctrine. It stands alone as good teaching. It is reiterated by Paul in Gal. 6:6 and First Tim. 5:17–18. But we are looking at the *agape* love continuing from chapter 8. That love shows itself in providing for the teachers of the Gospel. Then, Paul goes on with the subject of love.

> For though I am free from all, I have made myself a servant to all, that I might win more of them. To the Jews I became as a Jew, in order to win Jews. To those under the law I became as one under the law (though not being myself under the law) that I might win those under the law. To those outside the law I became as one outside the law (not being outside the law of God but under the law of Christ) that I might win those outside the law. To the weak I became weak, that I might win the weak. I have become all things to all people, that by all means I might save some. I do it all for the sake of the gospel, that I may share with them in its blessings.

Paul is so concerned for others that he will be a Jew to the Jews, a Gentile to the Gentiles, and weak to the weak. He will do whatever he has to do to share the Gospel with others (within the boundaries of proper Christian liberty). That is the love that Paul exhorts the Corinthians to have. And when you look at *agape* love, that is what you find. *Agape* love is self-sacrificial.

When you look at chapter 9 and know what is coming in chapter 10, you will see that Paul is establishing his authority as one sent directly by God, to deal very harshly with the Corinthians in chapter 10.

In chapter 10 Paul goes back to the beginning of chapter 8, food offered to idols. First, in First Corinthians 10:1-5, Paul tells some of the history of the Jewish people in the Exodus from Egypt under Moses and how God took care of them. They sinned in the wilderness to the extent that God told them that they would not be allowed to go into the promised land. Instead, they wandered in the wilderness until all the adults died (instead of faithful Joshua and Caleb. In verses 6–12, Paul stated:

> Now these things became our examples, to the intent that we should not lust after evil things as they also lusted. And do not become idolaters as were some of them. As it is written, 'The people sat down to eat and drink, and rose up to play.' Nor let us commit sexual immorality, as some of them did, and in one day twenty-three thousand fell; nor let us tempt Christ, as some of them also tempted, and were destroyed by serpents; nor complain, as some of them also complained, and were destroyed by the destroyer. Now all these things happened to them as examples, and they were written for our admonition, upon whom the ends of the ages have come. Therefore let him who thinks he stands take heed lest he fall.

Paul had given the Corinthians a very direct and powerful warning. The Corinthians are doing the very same sins against God that the Israelite did. In the Exodus, God was so offended that He killed twenty three thousand at one time. Watch out, Corinthians! "Therefore let anyone who thinks that he stands take heed lest he fall" (verse 12). He also encourages them with that fabulous verse 13, "No temptation has overtaken you that is not common to man. God is faithful, and He will not let you be tempted beyond your ability, but with the temptation He will also provide the way of escape, that you may be able to endure it."

But Paul does not stop there. First Corinthians 10:14–18 states,

> Therefore, my beloved, flee from idolatry. I speak as to sensible people; judge for yourselves what I say. The cup of blessing that we bless, is it not a participation in the blood of Christ? The bread that we break, is it not a participation in the body of Christ? Because there is one bread, we who are many are one body, for we all partake of the one bread. Consider the people of Israel: are not those who eat the sacrifices participants in the altar?

Paul was telling the Corinthians that the source of God's sins were that, while supposedly fellowshipping with God Almighty by eating the manna that He supplied and drinking out of the Rock, which was Jesus Christ, and were able to eat some of the food that was sacrificed to Him, also sinned greatly against Him. Because of that, they did not enter into the Promised Land. Paul continues stating, in verses 19-22:

> What do I imply then? That food offered to idols is anything, or that an idol is anything? No, I imply that what pagans sacrifice they offer to demons and not to God. I do not want you to be participants with demons. You cannot drink the cup of the Lord and the cup of demons. You cannot partake of the table of the Lord and the table of demons. Shall we provoke the Lord to jealousy? Are we stronger than he?

Paul commanded the Corinthians not just to be careful with idolatry, or turn away from idolatry, but to *flee* from idolatry (First Corinthians 10:14). Did Paul think there is actually some power to idolatry? That idolatry can adversely affect Christians? Apparently, he did (remember that these are not just Paul's words, they are the words of Jesus Christ)! According to this, the "weak," in 1 Cor. 8:9–12 were not so weak. And the "strong" were not so strong. In fact, it was the other way around. The "weak" were wise and the "strong" were foolish. Paul talked about the Lord's Supper in verse 16. In verse 17, he said that we Christians are one with God because we partake in the sacrifice of Jesus Christ, just as the Jews, in Judaism, were one body in God because of the Old Testament sacrifices. This puts the focus on one body of Christ, in Christ. Then he goes on to say, in verses 20–21, "No, I imply that what pagans sacrifice they offer to demons and not to God. I do not want you to be participants with demons. You cannot drink the cup of the Lord and the cup of demons. You cannot partake of the table of the Lord and the table of demons." The ESV uses the word "imply" in verses 19. The implication is that the argument has already been established in the previous verses 14-18. This fact, that a Christian cannot partake of God's table and the table of demons, totally refutes what the Corinthians said in chapter 8. They said that there is only one God, and the idols are nothing. So food offered to the idols is offered to nothing; therefore, there is no danger or sin (chapter 8:3–6). Paul said that the gentile idols are backed by demons. Demons are powerful and have the power and authority of Satan behind them. They are nothing to fool around with. Not even Michael, the archangel, would stand up to Satan face-to-face (Jude 9). So we certainly should not. That is not to say we cannot fight demons in spiritual battle. We can, but only by the name of Jesus and by the fact that we are covered by His shed blood, giving Satan and his demons no legal authority over us. That means we don't fool with demons or things of demons or things sacrificed to demons.

Paul goes on to say, "Shall we provoke the Lord to jealousy? Are we stronger than he? 'All things are lawful,' but not all things are helpful. 'All things are lawful,' but not all things build up" (verses 22–23). The Israelites in the wilderness provoked God to jealousy. Is that really what we want to do? Are we wiser, stronger than God? We may be given the liberty to do anything, as we are not governed by the Law now that we are under grace. But it is definitely not beneficial to do anything that has to do with demons. It is not a sign that we are "filled with the Spirit" (Ephesians 5:18).

Then, in verse 24, Paul goes back to the subject of Christian love: "Let no one seek his own good, but the good of his neighbor." Not only keep from offending God, but keep from offending fellow Christians with things that are not beneficial.

Paul alludes to 1 Corinthians 10:13 when he says (verse 25), "Eat whatever is sold in the meat market without raising any question on the ground of conscience." If you don't know the meat was sacrificed to demons, don't worry about it. But Paul also warns about knowledge (verse 28), "But if someone says to you, "This has been offered in sacrifice," then do not eat it, for the sake of the one who informed you, and for the sake of conscience—"

Here Paul goes back to what the Corinthians may want to say, "I do not mean your conscience, but his. For why should my liberty be determined by someone else's conscience? If I partake with thankfulness, why am I denounced because of that for which I give thanks? (verses 29-30).

Paul finishes with the statement, "So, whether you eat or drink, or whatever you do, do all to the glory of God. Give no offense to Jews or to Greeks or to the church of God, just as I try to please everyone in everything I do, not seeking my own advantage, but that of many, that they may be saved. Be imitators of me, as I am of Christ."

Even if you do choose to participate in things offered to idols (demons) with your personal liberty, don't offend others. Choose Christian love rather than selfish desire.

This is not the only place in the New Testament that Jesus Christ gives direction on things pertaining to idols. In Acts 15, Paul called the first Church Council. He goes to Jerusalem to talk to the apostles still there and James, the half brother of Christ, who was also the head elder, or bishop, of the Jerusalem church. The subject that Paul wants to discuss, even argue, is the separation of Christianity from Judaism. Paul was the apostle called to the Gentiles. He was chosen for a special, separate task than the other apostles were given. Paul was chosen to demonstrate, in the progressive revelation of Jesus Christ, that Christianity is not contingent upon Judaism. Christianity came out of Judiasm, and was allowed to live it's infancy along with Judiasm to keep Rome from persecuting it. But God meant Christianity to be totally separate, to stand upon its own. This was not understood by the other apostles, although Peter had some inkling of it with Cornelius which he testified before this council in Acts 11:16-17. So Paul told the Jerusalem church what Jesus had given him to say, that gentiles did not have to become Jews to become Christians. Peter agreed with Paul. There was some pretty forceful communication. Then James conferred with the apostles and gave judgment. "Therefore my judgment is that we should not trouble those of the Gentiles who turn to God, but should write to them to abstain from the things polluted by idols, and from sexual immorality, and from what has been strangled, and from blood" (Acts 15:19–20). The gentiles were not to be bound by Jewish law.

The only things that Gentiles were to follow from Judaism were as follows:

- abstain from things polluted by idols. Note that this is anything having to do with idols, not just food.

- abstain from sexual immorality. This means to keep away from all sexual thoughts or activities outside of marriage. No exceptions!!

- abstain from eating meat from animals that were strangled, that is, animals that did not have the blood drained (or bled) out.

- Abstain from ingesting blood that has been drained out by others.

5

THE CRUCIFIXION
WITH PSALMS 22

Or
God's Timing to Help His People in Their Need

Just before Jesus Christ was arrested, He went to the garden of Gethsemane to pray. He knew the following hours would be the toughest hours that He would live through in His humanity. In Matthew 26:36–46, three times Jesus prayed approximately this same prayer, "My Father, if it be possible, let this cup pass from me; nevertheless, not as I will, but as you will." Was the prayer of Jesus answered? In other words, did He suffer terribly in His humanity or did His Father God temper that suffering when he was on the cross?

The twenty-second Psalms has been recognized to be a Messianic Psalms about the Passion of Christ.

My God, my God, why have you forsaken me? Why are you so far from saving me, from the words of my groaning? O my God, I cry by day, but you do not answer, and by night, but I find no rest. Yet you are holy, enthroned on the praises of Israel. In you our fathers trusted; they trusted, and you delivered them. To you they cried and were rescued; in you they trusted and were not put to shame. (Psalms 22:1–5)

In this passage, Jesus is on the Cross talking to His Father. He is asking why the Father did not answer His prayer on Gethsemane. He said, in His prayer, that the Father inhabited the praises of Israel; the leaders of the Israelite trusted in Him and You, Father, delivered them. But Jesus complained, You, Father, have not answered my prayer for deliverance.

Let's continue and find other Jewels that we don't see in the Gospels.

Psalms 22:6 states, "But I am a worm and not a man, scorned by mankind and despised by the people." We find the same kind of language in Psalms 69:20; Isaiah 50:6, 53:5; and Zechariah 13:6, and it is in the Gospels, but Jesus, in this passage, is described as a worm. This worm is not the normal word for worm. It is a special worm with a special use, which is obtaining the die for the color scarlet or crimson. The Hebrew word used here is pronounced *shaw-nee*'. The word is used twenty-six times in the book of Exodus in describing the scarlet color of cloth and/or thread to be used in the Tabernacle, in the curtain between the holy place and the most holy place, and in the high priest's clothing (purple and scarlet). It is used in Leviticus, Numbers, and Deuteronomy to describe how to cleanse and purify the items for worship of God. It is used in Isaiah 1:18 to describe our sin: "Come now, let us reason together, says the LORD: though your sins be like scarlet, they shall be as white as snow; though they are red like crimson, they shall become as wool."

Think about this. Jesus calls himself the worm from which the color scarlet, or crimson, is obtained. How is it obtained? By crushing the worm.

- It involves suffering. The 22nd Psalm portrays Jesus crushed figuratively, in His suffering!

- The color was used in the Tabernacle, the place where God would reside and be worshiped. It was also used to purify items used in worship of God. It was about God, especially Jesus Christ, the "once and for all" Sacrificial Lamb.

• Our sin was described as crimson which Christ's blood will wash as white as snow or as white as sheep's wool.

Psalms 22:7–8 states, "All who see me mock me; they make mouths at me; they wag their heads; He trusts in the LORD; let him deliver him; let him rescue him, for he delights in him!" This happened before Jesus was sent to Pilate. All the Gospels tell how he was treated and criticized during His suffering before and during the Crucifixion.

Psalms 22:11–13 states, "Be not far from me, for trouble is near, and there is none to help. Many bulls encompass me; strong bulls of Bashan surround me; they open wide their mouths at me, like a ravening and roaring lion." Jesus, in His humanity, continued to cry to the Father that He needed help! The bulls of Bashan were after Him. The land of Bashan went from the river Yarmuck, near the southeast end of the Sea of Galillee north to Mount Hermon. It is where the *rephaims*, or giants, originated, of which Goliath was one. Bashan was known to be good pasture land. The bulls of Bashan was a local saying of the herds in the Bashan area, describing them as being large and strong. The term was also used for the giants, the *rephaims*. We know the nature of bulls is to be very territorial, to violently protect their territory. The term is used, here, to describe the Jewish elders and rulers who led the people against Jesus.

Psalms 22:14 states, "I am poured out like water, and all my bones are out of joint; my heart is like wax; it is melted within my breast;" Think of how Jesus felt on the cross. He was so broken that he had no strength in His bones to support His body. The beating and whipping he received was so bad that His bones were torn out of joint.

Psalms 22:15 states, "my strength is dried up like a potsherd, and my tongue sticks to my jaws; you lay me in the dust of death." He had no courage or moral strength to continue resisting death.

Verse 16-17a states, "For dogs encompass me; a company of evildoers encircles me; they have pierced my hands and feet—I can count all my bones—" The dogs may be referring to the gentile Romans, which were the way Jews thought about gentiles. Or it may refer to the Jewish leaders. Paul called the circumcision, highly positioned Jews who opposed His ministry, dogs. More likely dogs referred to the Jews who were so influenced by their leaders that they became like wild dogs that sometimes attacked a herd of sheep. His whipping was so severe that it tore the skin in strips off of his ribs and other bones; this is where His precious blood was shed.

Verses 17-18 states, "they stare and gloat over me; they divide my garments among them, and for my clothing they cast lots." This is a direct reference to John 19:23–24: "they stare and gloat over me; they divide my garments among them, and for my clothing they cast lots."

Verse 19 states, "But you, O LORD, do not be far off! O you my help, come quickly to my aid! Deliver my soul from the sword, my precious life from the power of the dog! Save me from the mouth of the lion!" He continues to call for His Father God to help him, to no avail.

Verse 20 is an appeal, "You have rescued me from the horns of the wild oxen!" Jesus tells God that, in His past life of incarnation, His Father God had saved Him from suffering and death. Why not now?

The crucifixion itself—death on the cross came by suffocation. We breathe via our diaphragm and chest muscles. When one is crucified, all the weight of the body hangs from the chest muscles; when the person tires, the chest cannot expand and contract; the person dies by lack of oxygen—suffocation. There were two general ways that the crucifixion was accomplished. The first was to make it quick. The second was to make it last a long time.

- Quick method of crucifixion—the person to be crucified was beaten so much that he was almost dead before he was hung on the cross. This is the manner used with Jesus. Most of His suffering was before the cross. His body was so weak that when put on the cross, he died in a fairly short period of time, probably from between 9:00 AM and noon when the sun turned dark until 3:00 PM, when He died. When you look at the day of crucifixion, Passover

Friday, the day before the Sabbath, this way fit Scripture. First, Jesus blood had to be shed (Passover Lamb). We saw Jesus's weak physical state in Psalms 22. That weakness was the result of intense suffering and shedding of blood before He was hung on the cross. Second, He had to be removed from the cross and buried by 6:00 PM, the beginning of the Sabbath. Preparation for the Sabbath had to begin at 3:00 PM Friday afternoon.

- Long-lasting method of crucifixion—the person was not beaten and whipped just so that he would be healthy when he or she was hung from the cross. People lived on the cross for days this way. When the Romans conquered the Jews in 69–70 AD, millions of male Jews were crucified along roadways. Because the bodies were healthy when put on the cross, the chest muscles and diaphragm could be forced to make the body breathe for a much longer period of time than if the person were beat and whipped before crucifixion as Jesus had suffered.

The Jews, both leaders and general population, verbally attacked Jesus:

And those who passed by derided him, wagging their heads and saying, "You who would destroy the temple and rebuild it in three days, save yourself! If you are the Son of God, come down from the cross" (Matt. 27:39-40). So also the chief priests, with the scribes and elders, mocked him, saying, "He saved others; he cannot save himself. He is the King of Israel; let him come down now from the cross, and we will believe in him. He trusts in God; let God deliver him now, if he desires him. For he said, 'I am the Son of God.' And the robbers who were crucified with him also reviled him in the same way (Matt. 27:41–44)."

The two thieves—we know the story. One was saved by belief which was based upon faith which was based upon God's work of grace versus the other who made his decision upon the freewill and rebellion of man against God.

Jesus was sure to take care of His mother:

> but standing by the cross of Jesus were his mother and his mother's sister, Mary the wife of Clopas, and Mary Magdalene. When Jesus saw his mother and the disciple whom he loved standing nearby, he said to his mother, "Woman, behold, your son!" Then he said to the disciple, "Behold, your mother!" And from that hour the disciple took her to his own home. After this, Jesus, knowing that all was now finished, said (to fulfill the Scripture), "I thirst." (John 19:25–28)

What about His drinking the wine?

1. Jesus was carrying the cross to Golgotha. He was so tired that they made Simon, a Cyrenian, to carry it for him and offered our LORD wine mingled with myrrh, which is a drug. Mark 15:23 states, "And when they came to a place called Golgotha (which means Place of a Skull), they offered him wine to drink, mixed with gall, but when he tasted it, he would not drink it." He was still working our salvation.

2. When they arrived at Golgotha, they offered Jesus wine. Matt. 27:33–34 states, "And when they were come unto a place called Golgotha, that is to say, a place of a skull, They gave him vinegar to drink mingled with gall: and when he had tasted thereof, he would not drink." The "vinegar" is sour wine, or a poor quality of wine used by the poor. Gall is bile, a bitter substance. Jesus tasted it but did not drink it. He was still working our salvation.

3a. After Jesus was on the cross, He was mocked by the soldiers and offered "vinegar." Luke 23:36–37 states, "The soldiers also mocked him, coming up and offering him sour wine and saying, "If you are the King of the Jews, save yourself!" Many people think that this time that Jesus was offered wine is the same as given us in the next two times it is mentioned. This was probably Luke's mention of Jesus last minutes. He had completed His mission of being the best and final Sacrificial Lamb which took away our sins.

3b. Matthew mentions two times that Jesus was offered wine; this is the second time. Matt. 27:46–49 states, "And about the ninth hour Jesus cried out with a loud voice, saying, "*Eli, Eli, lema sabachthani?*" that is, "My God, my God, why have you forsaken me?" And some of the bystanders, hearing it, said, "This man is calling Elijah." And one of them at once ran and took a sponge, filled it with sour wine, and put it on a reed and gave it to him to drink. But the others said, "Wait, let us see whether Elijah will come to save him." This is the same as Luke 23:36-37.

3c. John writes about the same instance, although some think it is the fifth time He is offered wine. The soldiers parted His clothing. Jesus assigned his mother to John to look after. He knew that he had accomplished all that He came to do. John 19:28–30 states, "After this, Jesus, knowing that all was now finished, said (to fulfill the Scripture), 'I thirst.' A jar full of sour wine stood there, so they put a sponge full of the sour wine on a hyssop branch and held it to his mouth. When Jesus had received the sour wine, he said, 'It is finished,' and he bowed his head and gave up his spirit." This is also the same as Luke 23:36-37.

Jesus was offered wine at three different times, (1) on the way to Golgotha, (2) just after being hung on the cross, and (3) just before He died. Some Bible scholars think that Jesus was offered wine five different times, that the last three instances were separate and at different times. When the different contexts are studied, it seems that the different writers detailed different, but not separate, things, and that the last three times are the same instance.

It was finished. On that last time Jesus was offered the vinegar wine, He was free to take the wine, fulfilling the prophesy in Psalms 69:21, "They gave me poison for food, and for my thirst they gave me sour wine to drink." Jesus's work on earth was done, completed. He died. The earthquake occurred and graves opened up. The darkened sun (solar eclipse) completed its cycle. It was the ninth hour, 3:00 PM. Remember that the Jewish leaders asked that the legs of the three crucified people be broken to cause the suffocation which causes death because the body could not breath without the support of the legs. and the bodies had to be removed before 6:00 that evening, as the following day was the Sabbath. But Jesus, according to God's plan, was already dead, fulfilling the prophesy that His bones would not be broken per Psalms. 34:20, "He keeps all his bones; not one of them is broken."

We went over many of the prophesies fulfilled by our Savior's suffering and death. Other fulfilled prophesies:

- Isaiah 53:6 states, "…the LORD has laid on him the iniquity of us all."

- Isaiah 53:9 states, "And they made his grave with the wicked and with a rich man in his death," (the grave of Joseph of Arimathea).

- Isaiah 53:12 states, He "…was numbered with the transgressors; yet he bore the sin of many, and makes intercession for the transgressors."

- Deuteronomy 21:23 (Gal. 3:13) states, "his body shall not remain all night on the tree, but you shall bury him the same day, for a hanged man is cursed by God."

Question: Did Jesus actually ask the Father to forgive the Jews for giving Him the death penalty as the English versions say in Luke 23:34? Less than forty years later, the Jews were conquered by Rome. Galilee and Judea were demolished. This was the direct result of the crucifixion of Christ. Note that John did not note Jesus request for forgiveness. The Greek word translated in English as *forgive* is *to lay aside, to leave alone*. It could mean *to forgive*, as forgetting. But could also mean *to leave it alone*, as don't forgive. When Jesus petitioned the Father to leave the people alone, He actually forgave the people who crucified Him, both Jew and Roman (and technically current day Christians). But there was a tremendous cost for the unbelieving Jews who rejected Him. God the Father permitted the result of what they did come to them in the Roman destruction in 69–70 AD (You can read about this war in detail in Josephus, who did the "Benedict Arnold" thing during that war). Those people, as with all unbelievers, will, at the Judgement of the Great White Throne, be sent to hell because of their rejection. There is a price to pay for rejecting the free salvation from Jesus Christ.

Now I want to correct an error universally taught about Jesus on the cross and sins. Everyone I have heard teaching about the crucifixion, including me, has taught that Jesus bore the sins of the world on the cross, causing the Father to separate Himself from the Son, and that His baring the sins while He died, gave forgiveness to all who had believed God and who would believe, apparently because God cannot come into the presence of sins. This is not what the Bible teaches.

1. If the Father separated Himself from the Son, it would divide the Trinity, which is impossible.

2. Second Corinthians. 5:18–19 states, "All this is from God, who through Christ reconciled us to himself and gave us the ministry of reconciliation; that is, in Christ God was reconciling the world to himself, not counting their trespasses against them, and entrusting to us the message of reconciliation." This is about the sacrificial atonement of Christ for us in the suffering and crucifixion, imputing His righteousness to us so that we may be acceptable to the Father, followed by the resurrection. God was in Christ. There was no separation of the Father from the Son. The Bible states that God was in Christ. This does not mean that the Father inhabited Christ during the passion of Christ. It does mean that the Father was intimately involved in the passion of Christ.

3. Second Corinthians 5:21 states, "For our sake he made him to be sin who knew no sin, so that in him we might become (or be made) the righteousness of God." The

English word *made* is used two times in this verse. But there are actually two different Greek words, each interpreted to the English word *made*.

- The first word, about Christ, is pronounced *poy-eh'-o*, which means "*legally declared*." If an innocent person wants to take the punishment for a guilty person, and the court accepts the exchange, the innocent person, who never was associated with the guilty deed and did not bear the actual guilt, was declared guilty, even though he was totally innocent in every way. The guilty person, who was actually guilty in every way, was declared to be innocent. This is what 2 Cor. 5:21 means when it states, "For he hath made him to be sin for us, who knew no sin." He was innocent but declared guilty.

- The second use of the word *made* is pronounced *ghin'-om-ahee*, a totally different word. It does mean *made* or *become*. We, believers, "were made the righteousness of God" in Him. This refers directly to 2 Corinthians 5:17 (emphasis added): "Therefore, if anyone is in Christ, he is a new creation. The old has passed away; behold, the new has come." This new creature that we became at salvation is always forgiven, always acceptable to the Father, and cannot lose favor with God in any way. We should repent when we sin to restore fellowship with God, but when we do sin, we never lose favor with God because we are always forgiven. We were made the righteousness of God in our Savior.

CONCLUSION

We started this study looking at Christ's prayer at Gethsemane. We found in Psalms 22 that the Father did not answer His prayer, in spite of the fact that Jesus continually prayed throughout the beating and whipping that He received prior to the crucifixion, and during

His time on the cross. God never answered the prayer of petition to the Father that He be spared from this suffering. Jesus displayed His humanity in His continual prayer. But, even while He kept praying to be released from the suffering, He submitted to it.

The following is directly related to that time of suffering and crucifixion and what we found in Psalms 22. Hebrews 5:7–9 states (emphasis added), "In the days of his flesh, Jesus offered up prayers and supplications, with loud cries and tears, to him who was able to save him from death, and he was heard because of his reverence. Although he was a son, he learned obedience through what he suffered. And being made perfect, he became the source of eternal salvation to all who obey him," This passage says, in verse 7, that the Father heard the prayer that Jesus prayed, in Gethsemane and throughout His passion that he be spared from the suffering and crucifixion. But, in spite of the fact given here that the Father heard the prayer, Jesus still suffered and died! Is the Bible lying? Did the Father actually the prayers? Maybe we don't know the whole truth?

In Psalms 22, we saw that the prayer for deliverance that Jesus continually prayed to Father God *was not* answered. In this Hebrews passage, we see that the prayer *was* answered. Jesus did die, but what happened a few days later? The resurrection happened!

- The prayer was answered!

- The answer was not *what* Jesus wanted, and the answer was not *when* Jesus wanted, but the answer *did come*.

- And the result was far, far better than what Jesus asked for! It was the Father's will for us who believe.

Can we learn from this?

- Do we find that, sometimes we don't understand God and His ways?

- Do we sometimes find ourselves suffering without knowing why?

- Do we question God because He doesn't seem to answer our prayers?

- Do we find that sometimes we limit God and don't allow Him to be God?

We must *trust* God, even when we don't understand. He is always in control. His will is perfect. His love for His people, believers, is perfect. He always wants what is best for us and His kingdom. He always answers prayer. Trust Him.

- I believe that, knowing more than we did before, we can understand Him better, and are encouraged to love God more than ever before. We then feel more secure than ever before in our relationship with Him.

- We can know that, in spite of trials, tribulations, and doubts, God is in control.

- Because of the above, we are more able to be used as God's tools in His kingdom for His glory and for our relationship with others in witnessing, vibrant Christ living and studying our Bible, learning more about Him and understanding Him more our life walk, thereby living out the desires of God for us as we do His will.

6

THE CHRISTIAN'S
SABBATH REST

In the Old Testament, we learned about the Sabbath rest.

- God created the universe, including the Earth, in six days. He rested the seventh, not because He had to rest, but to set an example, a standard, for the crown of His creation, people.

- In the Ten Commandments, God gave to the people of Israel laws to help them to understand what God expected out of them and for them to give to the rest of the world.

- God gave the Fourth Commandment:

  "Remember the Sabbath day, to keep it holy. Six days you shall labor, and do all your work, but the seventh day is a Sabbath to the LORD your God. On it you shall not do any work, you, or your son, or your daughter, your male servant, or your female servant, or your livestock, or the sojourner who is within your gates. For in six days the LORD made heaven and earth, the sea,

and all that is in them, and rested the seventh
day. Therefore the LORD blessed the Sabbath
day and made it holy (Exodus 20:8–11).

So the Sabbath was the seventh day of the week, the day we
know as Saturday.

- God did more than that. He also gave sabbatical years,
  one year of rest out of every seven, and one more year out
  of every fifty (Jubilee system).

- The Sabbath was so important that one of the reasons for
  the coming great tribulation is because God's chosen people, the Israelites, did not keep His Sabbaths. The Sabbath
  was very important to God in the Old Testament.

But if it was so important in the Old Testament, why do most
Christians worship on Sunday? Even more important, why is that
Fourth Commandment the only one of the Ten Commandments
that is not emphasized in the New Testament? What does the Sabbath
mean to the Christian? Or, to put it another way, what should the
Sabbath mean to the Christian?

Every year, we celebrate the resurrection of our LORD and Savior,
Jesus Christ. Does Christ's resurrection have anything to do with the
Sabbath? Christ's resurrection has everything to do with the Sabbath!

To start, let's look at the word *Sabbath*. It is from the Hebrew,
Strong's # 7673. It means "to repose, to stop exerting, to rest."
Sabbath means *rest*.

What should the Sabbath mean to us, believers in the new dispensation, as compared with that of the Old Testament Sabbath. All of
the Ten Commandments were confirmed in the New Testament *except*
the Fourth Commandment. Why is the commandment of the Sabbath
missing? What does this have to do with the resurrection of Jesus Christ?

Matthew wrote something very interesting after Jesus died on
the cross. In the passage written in Matthew 27:57–62, Joseph of
Arimathaea asked for and received permission to take the body of
Christ off of the cross. It was important to get the body and bury
it quickly, as the following day was the Sabbath. Under Jewish law,
work was not allowed on the Sabbath. Therefore, things normally

done on other days were not to be done on the Sabbath, so those things, preparing meals, buying groceries, working in the vineyard, cleaning the barn, among other things, would be done on the day of preparation, which was Friday, the day before the Sabbath. Jesus was crucified on Friday, the day of preparation. The Sabbath started at 6:00 PM on Friday evening. If Jesus's friends were to prepare His body to be buried according to Jewish law, the body had to be prepared and buried Friday afternoon before 6:00 PM. And it was mostly done. (They did a rush job of preparation of His body, which is why the women came to tomb on Sunday morning. They wanted to complete the preparation of Jesus's body.)

Matthew 27:62–63 said, "The next day, that is, after the day of Preparation, the chief priests and the Pharisees gathered before Pilate and said, "Sir, we remember how that impostor said, while he was still alive, 'After three days I will rise.'"

Note what Matthew said. He said, "The next day, that is, after the day of Preparation." He did not say, "On the next day, the Sabbath." But he didn't.

He did say, "The next day, that is, after the day of Preparation." Is the Holy Spirit telling us, through Matthew, that the Sabbath day, as a day set aside per the Fourth Commandment, had no more meaning or significance?

A real simple verse from First Corinthians 16 can begin to answer the question. Paul was talking to the Corinthians about giving.

- First Corinthians 16:2 states, "On the first day of every week, each of you is to put something aside and store it up, as he may prosper, so that there will be no collecting when I come."

Paul told them to lay aside the money they want to give for the Lord's work, and bring it to the Sunday worship service. Most conservative commentaries agree that, shortly after Pentecost, Christians had stopped worshiping on the Sabbath and had switched to Sunday corporate worship. In the Bible, you will find them in the Temple or synagogue on the Sabbath, but to witness and give testimony about Jesus Christ, not to worship Him.

But there is more. Please look at Psalm 118. In this Psalm, David is praising God for helping David in his victories against his enemies. Maybe we can see something more than that. David is talking about God's greatness in his life. He also prophesied about the greatness of the life of our Lord in the resurrection. Psalm 118 is generally recognized as one of the many Messianic passages in the Psalm. Let's take a close look at some portions of the chapter.

Verses 20 state, "This is the gate of the LORD; the righteous shall enter through it."

David mentions the Gate of Righteousness. He said that this Gate of the Lord, which is symbolic for Jesus Christ and His sacrificial suffering and death, makes it possible for those who believe to receive salvation and enter into fellowship with God for eternity.

In John 10:7, Jesus states, "Truly, truly, I say to you, I am the door of the sheep."

In verse 9, John quotes Jesus saying, "I am the door. If anyone enters by me, he will be saved and will go in and out and find pasture." The Greek word translated "door" in John 10 means entrance or portal. In common usage, it also means gate.

We can go back to Psalm 118:21, where David states: "I thank you that you have answered me and have become my salvation." Jesus Christ, by His death and resurrection, has become the salvation for all who believe!

Verse 22 states, "The stone which the builders refused is become the head stone of the corner." What can this stone be but Jesus Christ? The New Testament refers directly to this verse 6 times in Matthew 21:42; Mark 12:10; Luke 20:17; Acts 4:11; First Corinthians 10:4; Ephesians 2:20; and First Peter 2:4, 7–8.

Let's skip to Psalm 118:27: "The LORD is God, and he has made his light to shine upon us." Who is that light? John, talking about Jesus, in John 1:4–5, tells us who the light is: "In him was life, and the life was the light of men. The light shines in the darkness, and the darkness has not overcome it."

Then verse 27 goes on: "Bind the festal sacrifice with cords, up to the horns of the altar!" In the Old Testament sacrifice, the lamb or other animal was lead, on a leash or cord, to one of the horns of the alter, then killed. Christ was bound to the cross by nails, to die as the perfect sacrificial lamb.

Going back to verses 23–24 we see that, "This is the LORD's doing; it is marvelous in our eyes. This is the day that the LORD has made; let us rejoice and be glad in it."

"This is the day that the LORD has made." This is a prophecy about the day Christ arose from the dead. The work of the atonement of Jesus Christ, which included His suffering and death, was not complete until the Resurrection. The resurrection was the Victory. It was God's power over death; God had victory over Satan and sin. That's why we celebrate the resurrection even more than we celebrate Maundy Thursday, on which we remember when Christ was arrested, and Good Friday, the day we commemorate when He was beaten so terribly, had shed His blood by which we are washed clean from our sin, and was crucified as the final, perfect and prophesied Passover Lamb. The resurrection was the victory; it was very marvelous in the eyes of the Father, and should also be in ours. We believers, if we truly understand what Jesus had done, do rejoice and are glad in His atoning sacrifice. That is the reason why Christians started, soon after the crucifixion and resurrection, to worship on Sunday instead of on Saturday.

- Sunday is the day of worship for the Christian and has been since soon after the resurrection of Christ, according to writings of the period.

- We rest on Sunday, not because that day was made the Sabbath, but to honor the saving work of our Lord and Savior, Jesus Christ.

Personal questions for meditation:

- Do we praise God for what Jesus Christ has done?

- Do we exalt Him in the presence of others, believers and unbelievers?

- Do we witness to others? And are we willing to lead others to Him?

"Oh give thanks to the LORD, for he is good; for his steadfast love endures forever!" (Psalm 118:29).

Remember what Sabbath means. It means rest. It is a God-given and ordained rest.

Did Sunday become the Sabbath day, or has the Sabbath day been completely replaced by something else?

The first theological fact that we need to recognize is that the Sabbath was part of the Mosaic Covenant with God's chosen people. The only gentiles that were part of that covenant were those that were drafted, proselytized, into God's chosen people by being baptized (figuratively cleansed) into Judaism and those who lived with the Hebrews as slaves and friends, who had to agree to live by the laws of Judaism. The Church has never been part of the Mosaic Covenant, although some congregations and denominations believe in the replacement theology heresy that states that the Church has taken the place of the Israelites as God's chosen people.

- Exodus 31:16 states, "Therefore *the people of Israel* shall keep the Sabbath, observing the Sabbath throughout their generations, as a covenant forever."

- Leviticus 24:8 states, "Every Sabbath day Aaron shall arrange it (the showbread and frankincense) before the LORD regularly; it is from *the people of Israel as a covenant forever.*"

- Isaiah 56:6 states, "And the *foreigners who join themselves to the LORD*, to minister to him, to love the name of the LORD, and to be his servants, everyone who keeps the Sabbath and does not profane it, and holds fast my covenant…"

But there is more to the Sabbath than we find in theSabbath as the seventh day of the week.

The promised land was part of the Abrahamic covenant. The Abrahamic covenant was given in several parts of Genesis from chapter 12 through chapter 22. In Genesis 22:18, God told Abraham, "and in your offspring (KJV "seed") shall all the nations of the earth be blessed, because you have obeyed my voice." This is recognized to be a Messianic passage. Paul wrote about that promise in Galatians 3:16: "Now the promises were made to Abraham and to his offspring. It does not say, 'And to offsprings,' referring to many, but referring to one, *And to your offspring,* who is Christ." The "offspring" in Genesis 22:18 is Christ.

> Therefore, as the Holy Spirit says, "Today, if you hear his voice, do not harden your hearts as in the rebellion, on the day of testing in the wilderness, where your fathers put me to the test and saw my works for forty years. Therefore I was provoked with that generation, and said, 'They always go astray in their heart; they have not known my ways.' As I swore in my wrath, 'They shall not enter my rest'" (Hebrews 3:7–11).

This is a direct quotation from Psalm 95:7–11. The Psalmist talks about the children of Israel after Moses brought them out of Egypt, and after they sent the twelve spies into the promised land. They turned their back on the promised land and on God because they did not trust God to give them victory over the giants and the walled cities.

- So God said they will not enter into His rest.
- Why didn't God say that they won't enter into the promised land?
- God had something else in mind when He used the word *rest*.

In Psalm 95:11, quoted above in Hebrews 3:7–11, God told the people of Israel that there was another rest that they would not be able to enter into if they hardened their hearts like the generation that left Egypt. There was another rest that God had promised through the Abrahamic covenant, which would not be realized until after Pentecost.

Hebrews 4 begins with, "Therefore, while the promise of entering his rest still stands, let us fear lest any of you should seem to have failed to reach it. For good news came to us just as to them, but the message they heard did not benefit them, because they were not united by faith with those who listened" (verses 1-2).

Hebrews 4:9–11 states, "So then, there remains a Sabbath rest for the people of God, for whoever has entered God's rest has also rested from his works as God did from his. Let us therefore strive to enter that rest, so that no one may fall by the same sort of disobedience."

Please note that the focus that the writer is giving us is that the Christians' rest is a rest from his or her own works to please God (religion rather than faith). The tense of verse 9 *remains* is present passive indicative. *Present* means "now," whenever "now" happens to be. *Passive* means that it is of God's grace rather than our own work or decision. *Indicative* means that it is fact, not to be questioned. That means that the rest is not just eternity with God. This rest can and should be now, the present time! We don't have to wait until eternity! The promised *rest* can be right now, if we choose and obey with faith.

Paul also writes that we Gentiles of faith would also be able to enter into that rest promised in the Abrahamic covenant, not the Old Testament rest for Israelites that is the land, but to be in the rest of being children of God by faith.

- Galatians 3:26–29 states, "For in Christ Jesus you are all sons of God, through faith. For as many of you as were baptized into Christ have put on Christ."

To reiterate what we just went through,

- There remains a rest for the Church, believers in Jesus Christ.

- To enter into that rest, a believer must cease from his or her *works*, which means he or she must depart from his or her own unregenerated freewill, or self will or self-centeredness, all are the same. Our *works* are what we do to try to please God, done under our unregenerated freewill, apart from grace.

- We have to labor to enter into that rest. But it cannot be labor of our own will. It has to be because we have become slaves to God, taking His will upon ourselves as our own, denying ourselves (Gal. 2:20), and living by His grace, power, and authority.

So what is rest for the Christian? Is it Jesus Christ? It should be, but most Christians do not have that rest, it is most often that we don't have that rest in Jesus Christ. Can it and should it be, for all Christians? "Yes."

For the Christian who does not live by grace, there is not God's rest on earth, even if there will be rest for eternity in heaven. Remember that the first generation of Hebrews out of Egypt did not go into the promised land because of their disobedience and lack of faith.

I want you to know, brothers, that our fathers were all under the cloud, and all passed through the sea, and all were baptized into Moses in the cloud and in the sea, and all ate the same spiritual food, and all drank the same spiritual drink. For they drank from the spiritual Rock that followed them, and the Rock was Christ. Nevertheless, with most of them God was not pleased, for they were overthrown in the wilderness. Now these things took place as examples for us, that we might not desire evil as they did. Do not be idolaters as some of them were; as it is written, "The people sat down to eat and drink and rose up to play." We must not indulge in sexual immorality as some of them did, and twenty-three thousand fell in a single day. We must not put Christ to the test, as some of them did and were destroyed by serpents, nor grumble, as some of them did and were destroyed by the Destroyer. Now these things happened to them as an example, but they were written down for our instruction, on whom the end of the ages has come. Therefore let anyone who thinks that he stands take heed lest he fall. No temptation has overtaken you that is not common to man. God is faithful, and he will not let you

be tempted beyond your ability, but with the temptation
he will also provide the way of escape, that you may be
able to endure it (First Corinthians 10:1–13).

Is this to say that a true, born-again, saved, baptized Christian does
not have faith? No, it takes faith to be saved, through grace (Ephesians
2:8–9). I am saying that the vast majority of Christians do not spend
enough time with God in Bible, prayer and meditation, to even be
aware that there is a more intensive, intimate, rewarding life with God
than we understand. Instead, many pretend to have it through stirring
up high emotions, lively praise worship, etc, which form of worship
is a poor shadow of what God really has for us. Others spend lots
of time together in partially carnal, partially Christian compromised
fellowship, ignoring the fact that God has more in store. Others just
go about by including the false worship of extra-biblical or unbiblical
actions, such as a multitude of *baptisms of the Spirit* (the only baptism
of the Spirit is salvation), or as they have worshiped for years, knowing
something is lacking, but not knowing what to do about it.

Do you feel like a failure in your Christian walk because you
don't seem to feel real joy unless you get emotionally involved, where
you get worked up, the feelings flow, and you think you are having
an experience with Christ. But when the feelings are back to normal,
you can't restore that *experience*. That's because all those forms of
worship are false imitations of the true joy that Christ wants to give
you. Could it be that the heavy emotionalism of so many worship
services is actually Satan's work to keep God's people to reach the real
Sabbath rest that He has for us?

Matthew 11:28–30 states, "Come to me, all who labor and are
heavy laden, and I will give you rest. Take my yoke upon you, and
learn from me, for I am gentle and lowly in heart, and you will find
rest for your souls. For my yoke is easy, and my burden is light."

We tend to think that the word *rest*, in this passage, is talking
about a time to relax, spiritually and mentally, and refocus our lives.
That is not what it means. God has a very special meaning for that
word *rest*.

If we yield to Jesus and let His Holy Spirit truly guide and
empower us, thereby enabling us to live by grace, then Jesus Christ

becomes our Sabbath rest. He gives to us His will and fills us with His Spirit, if we ask Him to, in submission.

That is why there is no longer any Sabbath day. Jesus Christ wants to be, promised to be, our Sabbath rest. Sunday is our day of worship and should be spent to worship Him, in the fellowship of other believers in the local church, and to honor Him, because we celebrate His resurrection on Sunday. Our Sabbath rest should be Jesus Christ, Himself, not a day of the week. We just need to yield to Him totally. Our rest is a state of being in Christ rather than a day of observation.

HOW DO WE DO THAT? HOW DOES JESUS CHRIST BECOME OUR SABBATH REST?

Simeon Peter, a servant and apostle of Jesus Christ, To those who have obtained a faith of equal standing with ours by the righteousness of our God and Savior Jesus Christ: May grace and peace be multiplied to you in the knowledge of God and of Jesus our Lord. His divine power has granted to us all things that pertain to life and godliness, through the knowledge of him who called us to his own glory and excellence, by which he has granted to us his precious and very great promises, so that through them you may become partakers of the divine nature, having escaped from the corruption that is in the world because of sinful desire. (Second Peter 1:1–4)

The word *knowledge* is mentioned two times in this passage. The words *know, knowing,* and *knowledge* are used many times in the Bible. But here in 2 Peter 1, the word translated "knowledge" is a very special word. It is from the Greek word transliterated "epignosis." Gnosis is the root word which is the most common Greek word translated know, knowing, or knowledge. It means common knowledge sometimes knowing by what we have learned by experience (we learn to know "hot" by feeling it). We have experienced the Holy Spirit through salvation and through the Word of God. The word for knowledge that is used three times in Second Peter 1 is *epignosis* which is an form of the word knowledge, used in verses 2,3 and 8, also in 2:20. Spiros Zodhiates, in his THE COMPLETE WORDSTUDY DICTIONARY NEW TESTAMENT (Word Bible Publishers, Inc., Iowa Falls, Iowa,1992, page 624, states about *epignosis*, "It is more intensive than *gnosis*, knowledge, because it expresses a more thorough participation in the acquiring of knowledge on the part of the learner. In the NT, it often refers to knowledge which very powerfully influences the form of religious life, a knowledge laying claim to personal involvement." It can only be obtained by spending a lot of time with Him through the Word, prayer, and submission. With this abundant personal relationship with our LORD, God furnishes His power (v. 4), which is from the Greek word which our word *dynamite* comes from. This is not just a little bit of power we are talking about. It is God's awesome power! That power is available with the *epignosis* relationship. Look at the rest of verse 4. Through that intensive and intimate relationship with God, He gives us all things that pertain to life and godliness through that knowledge. The Greek word translated *life* here means an abundant, full life, meaning a vibrant personal relationship with Him; refer to John 10:10b, 15:8–16.

Continue to look at verse 4. Through this *epignosis* relationship, God also gives us "his precious and very great promises, so that through them you may become partakers of the divine nature, having escaped from the corruption that is in the world because of sinful desire." God gives us the ability to live a Christ-centered, Godly life in Christ through that relationship. We can actually escape the desires of worldliness that continuously try to overtake us. That worldly desires is all about *freewill* as compared to *grace*. Equate worldly desires with *self-centered freewill*. We are freed from that freewill (worldly and/or self-centered desires) in a vibrant, personal relationship with Jesus Christ through the Word, through prayer, and through obedience, thereby taking upon ourselves by our Christ-centered will, His desires, as our own. There is no room in a Christian's life for self-centeredness, which, if you stop to think about it, is "original sin!"

How Is This Possible? How Can We Reach that Impossible Goal?

Peter said, in Second Peter 1:1, that he is a servant. This word, in Greek, is the lowest form of slavery, in which the slave is allowed to have no will of his or her own, but must take upon him or herself the will of the Master only.

Let's go back to that word *knowledge* used in Second Peter 1:4, *epignosis*, meaning a abundant, intensive personal relationship with Jesus Christ. This kind of relationship cannot come to us by us working for it. I want to interject a thought from Creation and eternity future at this time. Before Adam and Eve's sin, they worked. But, because everything was perfect, they enjoyed their work! In eternity future, we will work, and we will enjoy our work. Why did Adam and Eve, in the Garden of Eden, enjoy their work and why will we, in eternity future, enjoy our work? We will enjoy our work because, first, we will be perfect, and, second, we will be doing the work that God created us to do for His glory!

Let's apply that idea to now, in this life of sin and degradation. We must work before we can attain to it, by studying the Bible, learning it, understanding it, meditating on it, praying and obeying, all of which God created us to do! Philippians 2:12 tell us, "Therefore, my beloved, as you have always *obeyed*, so now, not only as in my presence but much more in my absence, *work* out your own salvation with fear and trembling" (emphasis mine). We can enjoy our activities of life and enjoy our abundant personal relationship with our Lord! But we cannot gain that abundant relationship with Jesus Christ by our own works, by our trying to please God by doing things that we, in our natural state and with our natural freewill, try to do for Him. The work that pleases God is only by those who are saved, and comes only by grace, God's work in and through us. And grace comes through our surrender, submission, self-emptying ourselves of ourselves, and becoming a voluntary slave to our Lord, recognizing that He is our personal Lord as well as Savior, laying aside our natural tendency to control our own life through our own corrupted freewill, and letting God work in and through us, replacing our self-centered freewill with His perfect will to be our own Christ-centered freewill.

> Abide in me, and I in you. As the branch cannot bear fruit by itself, unless it abides in the vine, neither can you, unless you abide in me… If you abide in me, and my words abide in you, ask whatever you wish, and it will be done for you… If you keep my commandments, you will abide in my love, just as I have kept my Father's commandments and abide in his love… These things I have spoken to you, that my joy may be in you, and that your joy may be full. This is my commandment, that you love one another as I have loved you. (John 15:4.7,11-12).

When our LORD Jesus Christ suffered and died for us, His absolute righteousness was given to us so that God the Father can fellowship with us. This perfect righteousness given to us is called *Imputed Righteousness*. Imputed righteousness does not make us actually righteous.

Please recognize that our submission, by His grace, is required for us to live in Him, and Him in us. If we reject that grace, we are telling Him that He is not our Lord. If He is not our Lord, who is? There are only two lords in this universe, Jesus Christ and Satan. Yes, one can be saved and have Satan as lord of your life, and many, many people who call themselves Christians do have Satan as lord of their lives. Romans 6:16 states, "Know ye not, that to whom ye yield yourselves servants to obey, his servants ye are to whom ye obey; whether of sin unto death, or of obedience unto righteousness?" Romans chapters 6–8 goes into this in detail. In our life walk, only when Jesus is Lord of our life, living in and through us, bearing fruit within and outside of us, can we know that we are saved! This is not to say that, when we slip and fall, we lose our salvation. But, as the Holy Spirit is the seal of our salvation, as promised to us in Ephesians 1:13-14), it is also His job to grow us in God's Word, which, by grace, by God's love, by the work of the Holy Spirit, we become more Christ-like in our lifestyle.

The Old Testament has a beautiful picture that pertains to what God wants of us, and which Peter alluded to when he said that he was a *servant of* God (2 Peter 1:1. This picture is in Exodus 21, as well as other books of the Pentateuch. The Hebrew welfare system is described. If a man is so poor that he cannot support his family or even live without help, he can become a slave of another Hebrew for a limited period of time. That period of time ends at the Sabbatical year of the Jubilee system, the one year in every seven years that the land is to be fallow, to rest. On the Sabbatical year, that Hebrew slave is to be set free and be paid for the work he has done, so he can start over, again. But look at Exodus 21:5-6: "But if the slave plainly says, 'I love my master, my wife, and my children; I will not go out free,' then his master shall bring him to God, and he shall bring him to the door or the doorpost. And his master shall bore his ear through with an awl, and he shall be his slave forever." The person has become a voluntary slave forever, because he loved his Master. We, in our natural state, are spiritually dead, like the poor Hebrew was poor almost to death (Exodus 21:2-6). But God saved us by Grace through Faith, neither of which is our own so that no one can boast. Why? Look at Ephesians 2:10: "For we are his workmanship, created in Christ Jesus unto good works, which God hath before ordained that we should walk in them." He created us to love and obey Him voluntarily.

THE CHRISTIANS' SABBATH REST

When we, by grace, decide to live a self-less life by giving up our own fleshly desires, and decide to actually *live* for Christ (abide in Him), then God, when He knows we are ready, will perform another miracle in our life, making it possible for Christ to live through us, making it possible for Christ's will to becomes our will, giving us the power to do His work with His power! This is how to achieve that abundant, vibrant personal relationship with Jesus Christ and enter into His rest. This is where we get those "precious and very great promises, so that through them you may become partakers of the divine nature, having escaped from the corruption that is in the world because of sinful desire" (Second Peter 1:4).

- This is where the true Joy and Fulfillment comes from (Galatians 5:22; First Peter 1:8)

- This is what John 15, living in the Vine, is about (Jesus said that this is when He calls us *friend* (John 15:14–16). It is what makes "obedience" intuitive and natural.

- This is what it really means to be a New Creature (Second Corinthians 5:17) and to be crucified in Christ (Galatians 2:20).

Dear fellow Christians, this is the only way to live a Christ-like life pleasing to our Lord! God wants us to become voluntary servants (slaves) of His. In doing this, we can become all that God has created us to be and intends us to be, and it is how we can receive the fullness of joy!

Believe it or not, this step into the superabundant personal relationship with Jesus Christ is just as real and noticeable as salvation was. It is a complete change in focus and in what is important. Our desires and whole way of thinking changes. It has nothing to do with anything the "experience" oriented worship of speaking in tongues and many other false *baptisms* has to offer. It is dying to self. It is becoming that new creature that God has created us to be, but that so few of us have become. I believe it is what is commonly called *Lordship*, living with Christ as actual Lord of our lives.

Are you willing? It takes work, but it is God's work as we yield to Him. It becomes pleasant and fulfilling, in spite of the trials and tribulations we go through. It is rewarding if we truly yield and, by grace, permit ourselves to walk with Christ in His work, in the yoke of Matthew 11:28–30. This is how we receive His Sabbath rest.

- Matthew 11:28–30 (emphasis added), "Come to me, all who labor and are heavy laden, and I will give you rest. Take my yoke upon you, and learn from me, for I am gentle and lowly in heart, and you will find *rest* for your souls. For my yoke is easy, and my burden is light."

Are you willing? God is! Life in Jesus Christ and Him in us is our Sabbath rest.

7

TRUSTING GOD

Most of us believe that God has a definite plan for believers. We not only believe that God has given us a roadmap of His way in the Bible for all believers, but many also believe that God has a specific will, or plan, for each believer. In that specific plan for each believer, we believe that God leads us at times in certain ways.

What are the ways in which God leads believers individually?

- Prayer and the Word of God in daily devotions.

- Circumstances affecting us.

- Counsel from wise, mature believers.

- Still small voice of the Holy Spirit in us.

- Voice of authority over us (local church leader, government, employer, etc.).

Some say to look for God's leading in at least three of the above ways to verify God's direction, to aid in our decisions. Wise counsel from mature believers is always said to be one of the best sources of God's direction.

- Proverbs 11:14 states, "Where there is no guidance, a people falls, but in an abundance of counselors there is safety."

- Proverbs 12:20 states, "Deceit is in the heart of those who devise evil, but those who plan peace have joy."

- Proverbs 15:22 states, "Without counsel plans fail, but with many advisers they succeed."

- Proverbs 24:6 states, "For by wise guidance you can wage your war, and in abundance of counselors there is victory."

Let's look at one of the examples of a New Testament Bible character God has given us.

In his third missionary journey, Paul had been in Corinth for one and one-half years teaching the Word of God to the Corinthians. He left Corinth to go to Syria. On the way, Paul stopped in Ephesus and stayed there for over two years (Acts 19:10). While in Ephesus, he received direction from the Holy Spirit to go to Jerusalem then to Rome (Acts 19:21). Paul then went to Macedonia to spend some time with areas he had visited before. Then he went south into Greece with plans to leave for Syria. Jews were waiting to kill him, so he went back to Macedonia, then sailed to Troas, in Western Asia Minor, then south to Miletus, just south of Ephesus. In all of this travel the Jews, who wanted to kill him, forced him from his plan to go to Jerusalem from Ephesus, where he was when the Holy Spirit directed him to Jerusalem. He did not go back to Ephesus because he wanted to get to Jerusalem for the day of Pentecost (Acts 20:15–16). While at Miletus, he called the Ephesian church elders to come meet with him. He told them, "And now, behold, I am going to Jerusalem, constrained by the Spirit, not knowing what will happen to me there, except that the Holy Spirit testifies to me in every city that imprisonment and afflictions await me" (Acts 20:22–23).

After leaving Miletus, Paul's ship headed toward Phoenicia, what is now Lebanon, and landed in Tyre. At Tyre, Christians, through the Spirit, were telling Paul not to go on to Jerusalem." (21:4). Paul and his companions returned to `the ship and went to Caesarea, which is on the Mediterranean Sea in Samaria. At Caesarea, they went to stay with Philip, one of the dispersed Christians who had been one of the deacons of Acts 6. Acts 21:10–11 tell us, "While we were staying for many days, a prophet named Agabus came down from Judea. And coming to us, he took Paul's belt and bound his own feet and hands and said, 'Thus says the Holy Spirit, This is how the Jews at Jerusalem will bind the man who owns this belt and deliver him into the hands of the Gentiles.'" When the Christians with Paul heard that, they strongly urged Paul not to go to Jerusalem (v 12). "Then Paul answered, What are you doing, weeping and breaking my heart? For I am ready not only to be imprisoned but even to die in Jerusalem for the name of the Lord Jesus" (verse 13). The Christians found they could not reason with Paul so turned him over to God in verse 14: "And since he would not be persuaded, we ceased and said, 'Let the will of the Lord be done.'"

Let's look at what we have learned will happen to Paul in Jerusalem.

- With the Ephesian eldesr: Acts 20:22–23 states, "And now, behold, I am going to Jerusalem, constrained by the Spirit, not knowing what will happen to me there, except that the *Holy Spirit testifies to me in every city that imprisonment and afflictions await me*" (emphasis added).

- In Tyre: Acts 21:4 states, "And having sought out the disciples, we stayed there for seven days. And through the Spirit they were telling Paul not to go on to Jerusalem."

- In Caesarea: Agubus the prophet, in Acts 21:10–11 states, "While we were staying for many days, a prophet named Agabus came down from Judea. And coming to us, he took Paul's belt and bound his own feet and hands and said, 'Thus says the Holy Spirit, 'This is how the Jews at Jerusalem will bind the man who owns this belt and deliver him into the hands of the Gentiles.'"

- Also in Caesarea: Other Christians, in Acts 21:12 stated, "When we heard this, we and the people there urged him not to go up to Jerusalem."

What do you imagine the mature Christians were thinking at this point? Did they think Paul was in God's will, or did they think he was being stubborn and was mistaken in thinking he was following God's leading?

Paul gave us a little hint of what his mindset was in Acts 20:22, which we already looked at, "And now, behold, I am going to Jerusalem, constrained by the Spirit, not knowing what will happen to me there." Paul said he was *constrained by the Spirit* to go to Jerusalem. Constrained is a verb of force. It can mean that Paul was forced by the Spirit, but more likely, he was pushed in a way that was not natural for him by the Spirit.

Maybe you have said, or have heard said, "The Lord told me to do" such and such.

Most of the time other people think, "Yeah, sure, right." We don't get direct communication from God like that and we doubt when someone else says they do.

Please turn to Colossians 1:9–12:

> And so, from the day we heard, we have not ceased to pray for you, asking that you may be filled with the knowledge of his will in all spiritual wisdom and understanding, so as to walk in a manner worthy of the Lord, fully pleasing to him, bearing fruit in every good work and increasing in the knowledge of God. May you be strengthened with all power, according to his glorious might, for all endurance and patience with joy, giving thanks to the Father, who has qualified you to share in the inheritance of the saints in light.

Let's look at Paul's prayer for the Colossians.

- asking that we may be filled with the knowledge of his will in all spiritual wisdom and understanding

- so as to walk in a manner worthy of the Lord, fully pleasing to him, bearing fruit in every good work and increasing in the knowledge of God

- be strengthened with all power, according to his glorious might, for all endurance and patience with joy

- giving thanks to the Father, who has qualified you to share in the inheritance of the saints in light

Let's look at the first point from Colossians a little closer. Be filled with the knowledge of His will. What does this mean? What is God's will?

- First Timothy 2:4 states, "who desires all people to be saved and to come to the knowledge of the truth." God's desire, His will is that all people accept Jesus Christ as Lord and Savior.

- Matthew 28:18–20 states, "And Jesus came and said to them, "All authority in heaven and on earth has been given to me. Go therefore and make disciples of all nations, baptizing them in the name of the Father and of the Son and of the Holy Spirit, teaching them to observe all that I have commanded you. And behold, I am with you always, to the end of the age." God's will for all people to be saved is the Great Commission. The Great Commission also includes another part of God's will, which is to teach them to obey God.

- Ephesians 4:1 states, "I therefore, a prisoner for the Lord, urge you to walk in a manner worthy of the calling to which you have been called," God's will is for each Christian to grow spiritually.

- Hebrew 10:24–25 states, "And let us consider how to stir up one another to love and good works, not neglecting to meet together, as is the habit of some, but encouraging one another, and all the more as you see the Day drawing near." This is also part of the will of God that all believers become part of a local church and attend regularly.

These and many other passages are the general will for all Christians. But does God also have a specific will for each Christian?

Matthew 25:14–15 states, "For it will be like a man going on a journey, who called his servants and entrusted to them his property. To one he gave five talents, to another two, to another one, to each according to his ability. Then he went away." The man going on a journey treated each person alike, didn't he? No, he treated each person individually. God does the same from us. He has given each of us each inborn talents. When we had surrendered to God in salvation and had started to study the Word and pray, he "switched on" one or more of these talents to be "spiritual gifts" mentioned in Romans 12, not to "do" certain things as much as having the motivation to do things that minister to the saints in the body of Christ, especially in the local church. He has given each of us ability to learn and gave us each specific experiences by which to learn. He gave each of us different spiritual gifts. None of us is alike. Each is different. Why? So we are each equipped to do specific tasks for the above listed wills of God.

- To witness the Gospel to others.

- To fulfill the great commission, lead others to salvation

- To teach them God's Word and to obey God's commands (discipleship).

- To grow to be the mature Christian He created each of us to be.

- To be a beneficial and working part of the local church.

Look at John 15:1–5:

I am the true vine, and my Father is the vinedresser. Every branch of mine that does not bear fruit he takes away, and every branch that does bear fruit he prunes, that it may bear more fruit. Already you are clean because of the word that I have spoken to you. Abide in me, and I in you. As the branch cannot bear fruit by itself, unless it abides in the vine, neither can you, unless you abide in me. I am the vine; you are the branches. Whoever abides in me and I in him, he it is that bears much fruit, for apart from me you can do nothing.

Does Jesus Christ say that there is one branch in Him and that branch is the church? Or does he say that there are branches, and those branches are individuals. We are part of the local church and the Body of Christ. But He created us individuals. He treats us as individuals. He disciplines us and encourages us as individuals.

Let's look back at Colossians 1:9–12. We tend to look at this passage as written to the local body and being all-encompassing for one body. But let's look at it as written to individuals.

- That I, [your name], might be filled with the knowledge of his will in all wisdom and spiritual understanding.

- That I, [your name], might walk worthy of the Lord unto all pleasing, being fruitful in every good work

- That I, [your name] increase in the knowledge of God.

- That I, [your name], be strengthened with all might, according to his glorious power, unto all patience and longsuffering with joyfulness.

- That I, [your name], give thanks unto the Father, which hath made each of us meet to be partakers of the inheritance of the saints in light

God wants each one of us to be filled with the knowledge of His will in all wisdom and with spiritual understanding. He wants each of us to learn His will for us individually. Second Timothy 2:15 tells us, "Do your best to present yourself to God as one approved, a worker who has no need to be ashamed, rightly handling the word of truth." The KJV starts the verse with the active command to *study*, which fits the context. God wants each one of us to walk worthy of the Lord in our life, following God's leading for ourselves as led individually, as well as corporately. This cannot be accomplished without diligently studying the Word of God.

God wants each of us to increase in knowledge of God. This word *knowledge* is the intensified form of knowledge meaning full, complete knowledge of experience. This means not only knowing Him through book-learning and sermons, but knowing Him through personal experience in daily devotions and in His leading us through experiences that He leads us into and through.

God wants each of us to "strengthened with all power, according to his glorious might, for all endurance and patience with joy." This means that He wants us to be strong by learning to lean on Him, by trusting Him.

God wants each of us to be habitually *giving thanks to the Father, who has qualified you to share in the inheritance of the saints in light.* Each of the saints mentioned in the Bible was an individual that God led individually. We are partakers of the same inheritance as they. God wants us to be led individually by Him too. It may be part of a team or not. But should never be without the fellowship of the Church.

In Acts, as we read earlier, Paul went into Jerusalem. James cautioned him to go through the ritual Jewish cleansing in the temple so the troublemakers could see that he was still a Jew (Acts 21:23–24). He was able to give testimony to the Sanhedrin (Acts 23). But in spite of all that happened, he was still arrested. Then look what happened.

Jews tried to kill him (Acts 23:12–21). The captain of the armed forces in Jerusalem sent him to the governor in Caesarea, Felix (Acts 23:22–24:21). Felix wanted to please the Jews, and he wanted Paul to bribe him (Acts 24:22–27). Although he did not find anything to keep Paul imprisoned, he kept him in prison for two years. Felix was apparently replaced by Festus. Festus also had a hearing and found no reason to keep Paul in prison, but Festus wanted to please the Jews by keeping him imprisoned. Paul, knowing that the Jews would find a way to kill him, appealed to Caesar (Acts 24:27–25:12). Neither Felix or Festus should have kept Paul in prison. Then King Agrippa came to town. He heard Paul and said that Paul should have gone free. But since Paul had appealed to Caesar, it was on record, and Paul would have to go to Rome (Acts 25:22–26:32).

Doesn't this all sound like Paul was out of God's will?

- Wise Christians strongly advises that he not go to Jerusalem.

- He was arrested even though he followed James's advice to go through the ritual cleansing.

- He was twice kept prisoner even though he should have been set free.

- He had a hearing from King Agrippa, who would have set him free.

- He had already appealed to Caesar to keep from being assassinated, so was sent to Rome.

- This all sounds like Paul was out of God's will.

What did God say about this? Before Paul was sent to Caesarea, Jesus appeared to him and said, "The following night the Lord stood by him and said, 'Take courage, for as you have testified to the facts about me in Jerusalem, so you must testify also in Rome'" (Acts 23:11).

Proverbs 3:5–6 states, "Trust in the LORD with all your heart, and do not lean on your own understanding. In all your ways acknowledge him, and he will make straight your paths."

Now look at Proverbs 3:7: "Be not wise in your own eyes; fear the LORD, and turn away from evil."

It is evil to be wise in our own eyes. God has specific plans in His will for each of us. We are all, if we are in His will, being used by Him in the way He wants. We are *pots of clay* created to do His will (Isaiah 64:8).

Paul was right in the center of God's will. He was sent to Rome. What happened? He was freed, but only after he was under house arrest for probably several years. During that time, instead of traveling and evangelizing, he was writing letters, encouraging churches. He gave us several important letters of New Testament during that time. No one thought he was doing God's will by going to Jerusalem. But he was right in the center of God's will.

We can be right in the center of God's will too.

- Daily time spent in devotions, including reading the Bible, meditating on it, and prayer.

- Total and complete submission to Him. Trust no matter what He puts us through. We are only servants, no slaves, to Him. In being submissive, willing slaves, we are gaining crowns in this life, and crowns for the future life.

- Knowing that the most important thing we can be doing in this life is bound up in the Great Commission. Let God place us where He wants, and be a witness. Disciple others when we have the opportunity. Be part of the local church.

8

The *Shekinah* Glory of our Lord Jesus Christ

In the Old Testament, God showed Himself as the Awesome God of Creation and Nature. I would like you to try to picture the glory and greatness of God in these parts of history that I would like to take you through.

Creation

- We first see God in Creation.
  - Genesis 1:1–2 states, "In the beginning, God created the heavens and the earth. The earth was without form and void, and darkness was over the face of the deep. And the Spirit of God was hovering over the face of the waters."
- He spoke creation into existence:
  - Psalm. 33:6 states, "By the word of the LORD the heavens were made, and by the breath of his mouth all their host."

- ○ Hebrews 11:3 states, "By faith we understand that the universe was created by the word of God, so that what is seen was not made out of things that are visible."
- ○ Second Peter 3:5 (emphasis added) states, "…the earth was formed out of water and through water by the word of God,"

The Flood

Genesis 6. God made the flood happen. He separated out Noah and his family to continue creation, and destroyed all other mankind. Think about Noah. God talked to him. The extraordinary part of this is that, in the midst of a sinful and unrighteous world, Noah was in tune with God enough to recognize when God spoke.

God told Noah that there would be a flood, and all mankind and all air-breathing animals except those that would be I n the arc will be destroyed, killed.

God told Noah how to build the arc, and what did Noah do? He started building the arc.

Picture Noah and his family building the arc, and other people watching, criticizing them for doing this strange thing. Most biblical scholars think that it had never rained up until the flood. Neither Noah or anyone else had ever experienced rain or flooding. But Noah did as God told him to do. Picture Noah witnessing to them about God's coming judgment, trying to warn them that a flood would come and kill them all. Picture all the other folks rejecting Noah's message and starting to get mean. When someone hears the truth, they can either accept it or reject it. In rejecting it, their heart gets harder. They become hard. They get real critical. There is no question in my mind that people became mean to Noah and his family.

Consider Noah's family. He had three sons; Noah and the three sons were married. Picture Noah and his family building the arc. No one quit the work to go with the other people who were making fun of Noah. All of Noah's family stayed with him. They all had a choice to make. They could either go with the other people, who were going by carnal common sense with the way the world had always been, or they could stay with Noah, who was living a godly worldview by faith. They stayed. Why? There are only two reasons that I can think of. First, they respected Noah more than they respected all the other people. Second, they must have had some kind of relationship with God. God showed Himself strong to Noah and his family.

These manifestations of God, in the Genesis creation account and in the flood, were very great and powerful but were not *shekinah* appearances.

The Web site http://www.gotquestions.org/shekinah-glory. html states, about the *shekinah*, "The word *shekinah* does not appear in the Bible, but the concept clearly does. The Jewish rabbis coined this extra-biblical expression, a form of a Hebrew word that literally means 'he caused to dwell,' signifying that it was a divine visitation of the presence or dwelling of the Lord God on this earth." That presence was a visible manifestation that could not be understood in any other way than that it was the presence of God.

The Law

The God of the Old Testament, Jehovah, showed His presence with the People of Israel, not as a person as much as an individual force. This visible presence was, at times, so strong and awesome that people thought they would die in that presence. When God gave the Law to Moses and the children of Israel, this presence was called the *shekinah* glory of God.

Shekinah is from the Hebrew word that means "to dwell." It means "abiding presence." It is taken from the Hebrew word translit-erated *shakan*, Strong's #07931, which means to abide, dwell, reside. In use with Jehovah God, it means the place that He is to dwell. Sometimes, in the Old Testament, He dwelt visibly in a way that the people could see that He was present, whether in a fire or cloud, as in the Exodus, or in an exceedingly bright light, as when He entered the Tabernacle and later, the temple.

Glory is from the Hebrew word transliterated *kabowd*, Strong's #03519, which means "heavy, weighty, honorable." It is used to por-tray "importance, honor, someone worthy of respect."

So *shekinah* glory means the "abiding presence of God who is worthy of honor and respect."

When God revealed His presence to the children of Israel, there was no question in their minds that He was present, and that He was worthy of honor and respect.

Let's look at some of the times when God showed Himself in his *shekinah* glory.

At Marah, the children of Israel complained because of the bitter water. The *shekinah* glory of God was seen. Exodus 16:6–7, 10 states, "So Moses and Aaron said to all the people of Israel, 'At evening you shall know that it was the LORD who brought you out of the land of Egypt, and in the morning you shall see the glory of the LORD, because he has heard your grumbling against the LORD. For what are we, that you grumble against us?'... And as soon as Aaron spoke to the whole congregation of the people of Israel, they looked toward the wilderness, and behold, the glory of the LORD appeared in the cloud."

In the passage, Exodus 19:9–20, God showed His presence at Mount Sinai.

- Verse 9 states, "And the LORD said to Moses, "Behold, I am coming to you in a thick cloud, that the people may hear when I speak with you, and may also believe you forever."

- God told Moses to tell the people to prepare for His presence. On the third day, God would come in the sight of all the people upon Mt. Sinai. God told Moses to set boundaries to separate the people from Him. If the people crossed the boundaries, they would be killed. Moses went down and prepared the people.

- Verse 16 states, "On the morning of the third day there were thunders and lightnings and a thick cloud on the mountain and a very loud trumpet blast, so that all the people in the camp trembled."

Picture this if you will. God caused a lightning and thunder storm along with volcanic action. The storm did not rain, and the volcano did not explode. They were under the control of God. Was there any more potent force than the lightning and volcano? But the storm and earth quaking all stayed in one place. The potent force behind all of this was Jehovah God.

- Verse 17-18 states, "And Moses brought forth the people out of the camp to meet with God; and they stood at the nether part of the mount. And mount Sinai was altogether on a smoke, because the LORD descended upon it in fire: and the smoke thereof ascended as the smoke of a furnace, and the whole mount quaked greatly."

The people could see, hear, and feel the effects of God's presence, but God, in His love, protected them from it all. Now, do any of you believe that anyone in their right mind would come near the boundaries God placed to protect the people from Him? They wanted to run away. They wanted no part of this action.

- Verse 19 states, "Then Moses brought the people out of the camp to meet God, and they took their stand at the foot of the mountain. Now Mount Sinai was wrapped in smoke because the LORD had descended on it in fire. The smoke of it went up like the smoke of a kiln, and the whole mountain trembled greatly."

God was getting ready to give the Ten Commandments. The children of Israel saw, felt, and heard the presence of God Almighty. They saw lightnings and saw the mountain smoking. They heard thunder and the noise of trumpets. The felt the earth move. They were afraid of the awesome presence of the Holy God. In the next chapter, Moses tells us that they did not even want God to talk to them, they were so afraid. God, in His visible and audible presence had come to give them the moral law, the Ten Commandments.

What was the purpose of God coming in His *shekinah* glory? He gave them no excuse as to Who He was and that the Law was to show the people how to please Him, as well as how to live better lives than others. God did this in love so He could meet with the people. But He went further.

THE TABERNACLE

Exodus 40.

The Tabernacle and everything that went in it is now completed. Moses had it all set up and the furniture set in place as God had instructed him. The people were gathered around. God came in His *shekinah* glory.

- Then the cloud covered the tent of meeting, and the glory of the LORD filled the tabernacle. And Moses was not able to enter the tent of meeting because the cloud settled on it, and the glory of the LORD filled the tabernacle. Throughout all their journeys, whenever the cloud was taken up from over the tabernacle, the people of Israel would set out. But if the cloud was not taken up, then they did not set out till the day that it was taken up. For the cloud of the LORD was on the tabernacle by day, and fire was in it by night, in the sight of all the house of Israel throughout all their journeys. (Exod. 40:34-38)

God's *shekinah* glory filled the tabernacle. It was so strong that Moses was not able to enter into it. That glory was visible to all as the cloud by day and a pillar of fire by night that had led them from Egypt.

Remember the meaning of *shekinah* glory. *Shekinah glory* means the "abiding presence of God who is worthy of honor and respect."

God not only came down to show them how to please Him through keeping the Law. God gave them the Tabernacle. The tabernacle had in it the arc of the covenant which had a lid plated with gold. That lid was the mercy seat, or the throne of God. On each side of the mercy seat was an angel, a cherub. Each was facing the other with their wings touching over the mercy seat. This was where God met the high priest year after year, covering the sins of the people. This was the place of the *shekinah* glory of God. This was where God met with His people and forgave the sins of the people so He could dwell with them.

God's *shekinah* glory was there to show His mercy and forgiveness at His meeting place with mankind.

SHEKINAH GLORY IN SOLOMON'S TEMPLE

Later, when Solomon had built the temple and dedicated it with a tremendous blood sacrifice, God's *shekinah* glory again appeared. We find this in 2 Chronicles 5:1–8, 11–14.

Picture the great temple, with gold covering on the roof so people could see it from miles away, was complete. Solomon and the priests were there. All the gold and silver instruments were in place, with the great wealth dedicated to God. The Israelite elders and priests were taking the arc of the covenant to place inside the holy of holies. The people were gathered around while the arc was being placed. Solomon and the people were sacrificing a tremendous blood sacrifice offering.

Verse 6 says, "And King Solomon and all the congregation of Israel, who had assembled before him, were before the ark, sacrificing so many sheep and oxen that they could not be counted or numbered."

The priests brought the arc of the covenant into the temple and placed it in the holy of holies. The mercy seat, with the Cherubim, wings outstretched, was on the arc. The priests came out. The temple singers were singing praises to God. The trumpet and harp players were giving praise to God with their instruments. This was a joyful congregation. They were dedicating the temple.

Start at 2 Chronicles 5:13: "and it was the duty of the trumpeters and singers to make themselves heard in unison in praise and thanksgiving to the LORD), and when the song was raised, with trumpets and cymbals and other musical instruments, in praise to the LORD, 'For he is good, for his steadfast love endures forever,'" The KJV adds, "even the house of the LORD."

Again, the *shekinah* glory of the Lord was connected with the arc of the covenant not only in the Tabernacle but also in the temple. Remember the lid of the arc of the covenant is the mercy seat, where God met with the high priest once a year to forgive the nation of their sins.

Psalms 80:1 states, "Give ear, O Shepherd of Israel, thou that leadest Joseph like a flock; thou that dwellest between the cherubims, shine forth."

This shows us the meaning of *shekinah* glory. When God appeared in His *shekinah* glory, He was at the mercy seat, between the cherubim, ready to forgive a nation that did not deserve forgiving. He continued to stay at the mercy seat. He stayed through sin and rebellion, up until the time Babylon took Judah away into captivity. Near the beginning of captivity, Ezekiel saw the *shekinah* glory of God leave the temple in a vision, as the people were worshiping idols. (Ezekiel 9-10)

Turn to Hebrews 1. The *shekinah* glory presence of God came again. He came, again, to sit at the mercy seat, the place where God met mankind to forgive sins. This time, He came to forgive sins completely, not just to cover the sins as in the Old Testament.

Read with me Heb. 1:1–2: "God, who at sundry times and in divers manners spake in time past unto the fathers by the prophets, Hath in these last days spoken unto us by his Son, whom he hath appointed heir of all things, by whom also he made the worlds;"

Now look at verse 3: "Who being the **brightness** of his glory, and the **express image** of his (God the Father's) person, and upholding all things by the word of his power, when he had by himself purged our sins, sat down on the right hand of the Majesty on high;"

Jesus Christ, when He came to earth as the sacrificial lamb, was the *shekinah* glory of God. He was the brightness of God's glory. Warren Wiersbe says "'brightness of His glory' refers to the *shekinah* glory of God that dwelt in the tabernacle and temple" (*The Bible Exposition Commentary*, vol. 2, Victor Books, 1989, Pg. 280, an "Exposition of the New Testament Comprising the Entire 'Be' Series). Hebrews 1:3 states that Jesus Christ was the "express image of his person." Warren Wiersbe says that this means Jesus Christ is the "Exact Imprint" of God the Father (ibid).

We saw God appearing to the Israelites in His *shekinah* glory. He made the way for mankind to approach Him, and for Him to forgive them. The Law was not adequate. Even in His *shekinah* glory, God was not seen in His complete glory and love.

Hebrews 1:3 says that Jesus Christ came in the brightness of His glory, the express image of His Person, when He came to earth to purge our sins. That brightness of God's glory is the complete, total *shekinah* glory of God.

The Old Testament *shekinah* glory was great power that was seen, felt, and heard.

The New Testament *shekinah* glory was Jesus Christ, come in humility to serve us (Phil. 2:5–11).

> Then I said, 'Behold, I have come to do your will, O God, as it is written of me in the scroll of the book.' When he said above, "You have neither desired nor taken pleasure in sacrifices and offerings and burnt offerings and sin offerings" (these are offered according to the law), then he added, "Behold, I have come to do your will." He abolishes the first in order to establish the second. And by that will we have been sanctified through the offering of the body of Jesus Christ once for all (Heb. 10:7–10).

Jesus Christ gave us His Completed Word (Luke 4:18). He died for us. He came to completely forgive, not just to cover our sins. He came to be our mercy seat, the meeting place, with the full grace of God.

Jesus, the Christ, started all this by coming to Earth as a baby, born of a virgin, prophesied by the prophets. He came to die so that we may live. He is the *shekinah* glory of God. He sent His Holy Spirit to dwell in us. He is present with us and in all who believe. He is God.

How can we Apply this Truth of Salvation

What if that free ticket to heaven was only given because of our testimony of God in our lives to others?

What if God asked our neighbors if we have shared the Gospel with them, and if they know we are Christians by the way we live?

What if God asked the people we live with?

What if he asked our grocer, plumber, friends, and other people we come in contact with?

If our ticket to heaven was dependent upon what others say about us, would we gain that ticket to heaven? If our getting into heaven was conditional upon having others who had known us telling God that we have shown that we were Christians by our testimony in order for us to get to heaven, would we still get there?

The testimony that we give to others in sharing the Gospel and in the way we live should be a direct result of salvation. It is the the result of the work of the Holy Spirit working God's Word in our lives. James says, tell me of your faith in Christ all you want.

> So also faith by itself, if it does not have works, is dead. But someone will say, "You have faith and I have works." Show me your faith apart from your works, and I will show you my faith by my works. You believe that God is one; you do well. Even the demons believe—and shudder! Do you want to be shown, you foolish person, that faith apart from works is useless? (James 2:17–20).

Are we living a life of obedience? Is the Holy Spirit working through us to influence others toward Christ? Is sacrificial love a governing part of our life?

Are we sharing the Gospel with others, being willing to lead them to Christ? This is part of the work of Christians. It is not voluntary. In fact, the lack of these things may mean that our salvation is a figment of our imagination. It may not be real. The work of the Holy Spirit in our lives is the proof of salvation. Rom. 8:16-17 exhorts us, "The Spirit himself bears witness with our spirit that we are children of God, and if children, then heirs—heirs of God and fellow heirs with Christ, provided we suffer with him in order that we may also be glorified with him."

9

A Study of the Vine and It's Branches: Part 1

The author is not a preacher. He is a teacher. Teaching often goes beyond areas where preachers tend to go. But a teacher's job is not to convict people of their sins, or to give an altar call every week, or to uplift people in times of trouble, although many teachers are quite capable of doing those things. The teacher's job is to explain, or expose, the Bible in ways that enable people to understand God's Word better, learn more about God and how He works, and learn more about ourselves and our place in God's kingdom, whether we know Jesus Christ as Savior or not. In explaining, or exposing God's Word, the Gospel comes through in many different ways because the Bible is a supernatural Book, working in many different, but perfect ways. Hosea, in chapter 6:6, told his people, "For I desire steadfast love and not sacrifice, the knowledge of God rather than burnt offerings." The particular Hebrew word translated "knowledge," as in "knowledge of God," means complete knowledge, discernment, and understanding. Teaching this full and complete knowledge is the goal of teaching. The teacher enables the student to know and understand the Bible, God's love letter to us.

Are any of you farmers? Raised on a farm? Have a garden? A benefit of being a farmer, even a hobby farmer, is the ability to eat of what the farm produces. But a farm, as a business, has a purpose that goes beyond feeding the owners. A farm has the goal of earning a profit. The Bible talks about this business in different passages. Let's look at some of them.

In Leviticus 25:3-4, Moses was teaching the Children of Israel the law of Sabbatical years. They shall work in the fields for six years, and let the fields rest the seventh. "For six years you shall sow your field, and for six years you shall prune your vineyard and gather in its fruits, but in the seventh year there shall be a Sabbath of solemn rest for the land, a Sabbath to the LORD. You shall not sow your field or prune your vineyard."

This passage not only limits the landowners to six years of working and gathering out of seven but also describes the work that is done. We can see that the work involves sowing the fields, then pruning the crop, and then the fruit can be picked. Psalms 107:37 states, "they sow fields and plant vineyards and get a fruitful yield." Not only can the fruit be picked and eaten, the fields and vineyards were to produce an increase."

Song of Solomon 8:11 states, "Solomon had a vineyard at Baal-hamon; he let out the vineyard to keepers; each one was to bring for its fruit a thousand pieces of silver." This vineyard of Solomon's had a purpose. It not only bore fruit that farmers produced enough for themselves and their family, but gained the owner an increase, a profit of a thousand pieces of silver" for the right to use the vineyard. *The vineyard was to be harvested to bring a profit.*

So what is the purpose of fruit-bearing plants, meaning any plant that is farmed?

- Multiply
- Be harvested
- The increase was to bring a profit.

God often used the occupation of farming for word pictures. God gave a word-picture of Israel as a vineyard of choice vines.

Let me sing for my beloved my love song concerning his vineyard: My beloved had a vineyard on a very fertile hill. He dug it and cleared it of stones, and planted it with choice vines; he built a watchtower in the midst of it, and hewed out a wine vat in it; and he looked for it to yield grapes, but it yielded wild grapes. And now, O inhabitants of Jerusalem and men of Judah, judge between me and my vineyard. What more was there to do for my vineyard, that I have not done in it? When I looked for it to yield grapes, why did it yield wild grapes? (Isaiah 5:1–4).

The passage is a word picture. What did the vineyard represent?

- It represented Israel, God's chosen people.

- He led them to a land that was a great land, the land of Goshen, in Egypt so that they could grow numerically.

- He let them suffer in slavery so they would grow together and be physically strong, by adversity, to become a nation.

- He led them miraculously out of Egypt and into the land He had promised to Abraham, Isaac and Jacob. It was a good land.

- And all He asked them to do was to obey Him, and He would make them the greatest nation on earth.

But did they obey Him? For eight hundred years, most of the time most of the people did not obey Him. That is what the parable in Isaiah 5 was about. Israel, who should have been like the most choice fruit on the planet, had become like wild grapes, instead, and continuing with the word picture, the wild grapes were no good except to cut down and burn.

Did God, the keeper, take good care of the vineyard?

He chose a very fruitful hill.
He fenced it.
He removed all the stones.

He planted the choicest vine.
He built a watch tower in it.
He put a workplace in it.

What did God expect out of the vineyard? He expected grapes worthy of his labor, a good harvest, and an increase on His investment. Did He get it? No.

Looking at what these word pictures from the Bible, which represents Israel, what did God expect from His people? He expected a return on His investment. He expected a profit. What was the profit that God expected out of His chosen people, the descendants of Abraham? He expected His chosen people to spread the goodness and greatness of their God to the rest of the world?

- Through the descendants of Abraham:
  - Genesis 12:1–3 states, "Now the LORD said to Abram, 'Go from your country and your kindred and your father's house to the land that I will show you. And I will make of you a great nation, and I will bless you and make your name great, so that you will be a blessing. I will bless those who bless you, and him who dishonors you I will curse, and in you all the families of the earth shall be blessed.'"
  - Genesis 18:17–19 tells us, "The LORD said, "Shall I hide from Abraham what I am about to do, seeing that Abraham shall surely become a great and mighty nation, and all the nations of the earth shall be blessed in him? For I have chosen him, that he may command his children and his household after him to keep the way of the LORD by doing righteousness and justice, so that the LORD may bring to Abraham what he has promised him.""
  - Genesis 22:18 states, "and in your offspring shall all the nations of the earth be blessed, because you have obeyed my voice."

117

- Through Isaac:
  - Genesis 26:4–5 states, "I will multiply your offspring as the stars of heaven and will give to your offspring all these lands. And in your offspring all the nations of the earth shall be blessed, because Abraham obeyed my voice and kept my charge, my commandments, my statutes, and my laws."

- Through Jacob:
  - Genesis 28:14 states, "Your offspring shall be like the dust of the earth, and you shall spread abroad to the west and to the east and to the north and to the south, and in you and your offspring shall all the families of the earth be blessed."

- New Testament:
  - Acts 3:25–26 states, "You are the sons of the prophets and of the covenant that God made with your fathers, saying to Abraham, 'And in your offspring shall all the families of the earth be blessed.' God, having raised up his servant, sent him to you first, to bless you by turning every one of you from your wickedness."

  - Galatians 3:7–9 tells us, "Know then that it is those of faith who are the sons of Abraham. And the Scripture, foreseeing that God would justify the Gentiles by faith, preached the gospel beforehand to Abraham, saying, 'In you shall all the nations be blessed.' So then, those who are of faith are blessed along with Abraham, the man of faith."

The Abrahamic covenant, given to God's chosen people, is brought into the New Testament, as seen above. In Acts, Peter brought the Abrahamic covenant into the New Testament with Jesus Christ, where Peter condemned the Jews for not accepting Him as the fulfillment of that covenant (Acts 2:22-23).

Now, God continued to use farming as a work picture to enable us to look at the different kinds of people in the Church Age, and which people are capable of bearing fruit for God.

> And he told them many things in parables, saying: 'A sower went out to sow. And as he sowed, some seeds fell along the path, and the birds came and devoured them. Other seeds fell on rocky ground, where they did not have much soil, and immediately they sprang up, since they had no depth of soil, but when the sun rose they were scorched. And since they had no root, they withered away. Other seeds fell among thorns, and the thorns grew up and choked them. Other seeds fell on good soil and produced grain, some a hundredfold, some sixty, some thirty. He who has ears, let him hear'" (Matthew 13:3–9).

In this parable, or word picture of the Soils, there are four types of soils. The farmer represents God in this New Testament dispensation, working His Holy Spirit through people who He would have accept Jesus Christ as Savior. The seeds represent the Word of God. The types of soils represent types of people who hear the Word of God:

- The way side, which is the hardened path that the farmer used to get around to different parts of the field—Matthew 13:19 states (emphasis added), "When anyone hears the word of the kingdom and *does not understand it*, the evil one comes and snatches away what has been sown in his heart. This is what was sown along the path."

- Shallow soil with bedrock under it—Matthew 13:20–21 states, "As for what was sown on rocky ground, this is the one who hears the word and immediately receives it with joy, yet he has no root in himself, but endures for a while, and when tribulation or persecution arises on account of the word, immediately he falls away."

- Soil with Thorns—Matthew 13:22 states, "As for what was sown among thorns, this is the one who hears the word, but the cares of the world and the deceitfulness of riches choke the word, and it proves unfruitful."

- Good, prepared ground that bore good fruit even to a hundredfold—Matthew 13:23 states, "As for what was sown on good soil, this is the one who hears the word and understands it. He indeed bears fruit and yields, in one case a hundredfold, in another sixty, and in another thirty."

What does it mean that the good ground bore fruit thirty-, sixty-, or hundredfold? We know that it simply means that the seeds that were invested into the business to bring a profit brought forth thirty, sixty, or one hundred times as much as the quantity of seeds that the farmer started with. So the farmer was able to take 10 percent of the increase back for the next year's investment, use some of the rest to feed his family and pay business expenses, and sell the rest for a profit, the profit that He labored for and expected.

What is the spiritual message that Jesus Christ was telling the people, and us, by this parable? He explained several things:

- First is that He expects a return on His investment from those who believe in Him.
- Second is that many people, if not most, will reject Him.
- Third is that those who are true believers will produce spiritual fruit, even to a hundredfold, returning back to God a profit on His investment, which investment was the salvation by Jesus Christ, offered to all.

We need to remember that God showers with grace each person who hears the Gospel. Salvation is God's work. He ordained it, empowered it and brings forth the fruit. His Word will never return void or worthless (Isaiah 55:11). If the person wants to reject God's grace, he or she will suffer for it, for that is not God's will.

The seed is the Word of God, often with personal testimony, given to others, accomplished by the power and blessing of the Holy Spirit.

The soils are different types of people, or the different reactions people give to the Gospel. No one is predestined by God's choice to reject their Savior.

- First Timothy 2:4 talks about God: "who desires all people to be saved and to come to the knowledge of the truth."

- Second Peter 3:9 states, "The Lord is not slow to fulfill his promise as some count slowness, but is patient toward you, not wishing that any should perish, but that all should reach repentance."

God is sovereign. He has the ability and power to rule totally. But He has purposed to give mankind freewill, and He will not tread on that freewill. Therefore, if a person wants to reject Him, God will not force him or her to accept Him. But that person must bear the consequences.

According to Luke 8:8, what does God really desire, or expect, from the fruit plant? (Much _increase_ even to a hundredfold).

In every Scriptural example we looked at, what do the plants represent? Nations or people.

Does God expect an increase from people and nations whom He has blessed with His Gospel?

God gives another type of picture of business to help us to understand His expectations of His people.

> For it will be like a man going on a journey, who called his servants and entrusted to them his property. To one he gave five talents, to another two, to another one, to each according to his ability. Then he went away. He who had received the five talents went at once and traded with them, and he made five talents more. So also he who had the two talents made two talents more. But he who had received the one talent went and dug in the ground and hid his master's money. Now after a long time the master of those servants came and settled accounts with them. And he who had received the five talents came forward, bringing five talents more, saying, 'Master, you delivered

to me five talents; here I have made five talents more.' His master said to him, 'Well done, good and faithful servant. You have been faithful over a little; I will set you over much. Enter into the joy of your master.' And he also who had the two talents came forward, saying, 'Master, you delivered to me two talents; here I have made two talents more.' His master said to him, 'Well done, good and faithful servant. You have been faithful over a little; I will set you over much. Enter into the joy of your master.' He also who had received the one talent came forward, saying, 'Master, I knew you to be a hard man, reaping where you did not sow, and gathering where you scattered no seed, so I was afraid, and I went and hid your talent in the ground. Here you have what is yours.' But his master answered him, 'You wicked and slothful servant! You knew that I reap where I have not sowed and gather where I scattered no seed? Then you ought to have invested my money with the bankers, and at my coming I should have received what was my own with interest. So take the talent from him and give it to him who has the ten talents. For to everyone who has will more be given, and he will have an abundance. But from the one who has not, even what he has will be taken away. And cast the worthless servant into the outer darkness. In that place there will be weeping and gnashing of teeth' (Matthew 25:14–30)

The servant who was given five talents invested the five wisely, gaining 100 percent increase. This servant knew his master and understood his master's expectation.

The servant who was given two talents invested wisely, also gaining 100 percent increase. This servant also knew his master and understood his master's expectation.

Because of this, the Master promised both of them greater responsibilities and rewards. "His master said to him, 'Well done, good and faithful servant. You have been faithful over a little; I will set you over much. Enter into the joy of your master.'

The servant to whom the Master invested one talent did not trust his Master but was afraid of him. So, in fear of losing the talent entrusted to him, he hid the money. "But his master answered him, 'You wicked and slothful servant! You knew that I reap where I have not sowed and gather where I scattered no seed? Then you ought to have invested my money with the bankers, and at my coming I should have received what was my own with interest" (Matthew 25:26-27). Was the master unfair? No. Two of the three servants knew and understood what the master wanted and accomplished the task successfully.

The Master told the untrustworthy man who gained zero increase that he should at the very least have gotten a few percent interest rather than hiding the money. The Master wanted a return on His investment but did not get any. Note that the Master said that this servant was *unprofitable*. God wants us to be profitable in His kingdom, doing His work.

We go on with the passage. "So take the talent from him and give it to him who has the ten talents. For to everyone who has will more be given, and he will have an abundance. But from the one who has not, even what he has will be taken away. And cast the worthless servant into the outer darkness. In that place there will be weeping and gnashing of teeth" (Matthew 25:28-30).

The servant in whom the Master invested ten talents and brought forth 100 percent profit was given the one talent as a bonus for doing well. Jesus said that those who have shall be given more and shall have abundance. This is talking about the benefits of living in Christ. It is talking about spiritual fruit given in Galatians 5:22–23: "But the fruit of the Spirit is love, joy, peace, patience, kindness, goodness, faithfulness, gentleness, self-control; against such things there is no law." It is given for being obedient.

The wicked servant was put into the outer part of the Master's court, with no responsibility and no rewards, no joy, no close companionship with the Master or with those who did the Master's work faithfully. He was an unprofitable servant. Note that this person did not cease to be a servant. Looking at it from a more spiritual viewpoint, this person did not lose his salvation. He was kicked out of the banquet hall, in which was the presence of God and full fellowship with Jesus Christ and believers who are faithful to their Master. He was put into the outer part of the court, where it was dark and dreary. But he was still in God's mansion. He was separated from his Master because he lived by his own thinking, his own freewill, rather than by grace, God working in and through him. He did not please his Master, which is sin.

Please take note that the two servants who produced a profit for their master accomplished it by trusting and relying on their Master. The servant who hid the money did not trust and rely upon his Master. He relied upon himself and therefore was worthless.

This is pictured to us in a couple of passages from the New Testament.

- Romans 6:16 states, "Do you not know that if you present yourselves to anyone as obedient slaves, you are slaves of the one whom you obey, either of sin, which leads to death, or of obedience, which leads to righteousness?"

- Matthew 6:24 states, "No one can serve two masters, for either he will hate the one and love the other, or he will be devoted to the one and despise the other. You cannot serve God and money [or worldly values]."

The believer who is not bearing fruit may be excommunicated or barred from fellowship in the local church, put out where Satan can buffet him, and hopefully repentance come. But he does not lose his salvation.

The others pleased their Master, which is more than the imputed righteousness of salvation, it is actual righteousness which comes from loving their Lord and obeying Him. John 15:10, 14 tells us, "If you keep my commandments, you will abide in my love, just as I have kept my Father's commandments and abide in his love... you are my friends if you do what I command you."

Is it selfish for God to want a return on his investment from people who are believers? Is it wrong for God to expect a profit? Absolutely not! For one thing, God is perfect. He is so perfect that He has limitations. He cannot do anything that is not perfect. He cannot do anything that is not the best for His people (Rom. 8:28). He is so perfect that He can do nothing wrong. Such limitations! I wish we believers had such limitations! (But, in fact, we do, if we just live in Christ, Gal. 2:20, 2 Peter 1:3–4.) He is so perfect that He cannot wish for anything less than that unbelievers would become believers. God is not selfish to expect a profit from His people. And He has a wonderful plan for us believers, which is to grow spiritually to become like Him.

It is at this point that I have to ask the question, "Is anyone who may be reading this, me included, satisfied that he or she is as fruitful as God wants him or her to be?"

And the next question has to be, "Why not?"

Well, that was all introduction. Let's look at the passage of Jesus, the Vine.

> I am the true vine, and my Father is the vinedresser. Every branch of mine that does not bear fruit he takes away, and every branch that does bear fruit he prunes, that it may bear more fruit. Already you are clean because of the word that I have spoken to you. Abide in me, and I in you. As the branch cannot bear fruit by itself, unless it abides in the vine, neither can you, unless you abide in me. I am the vine; you are the branches. Whoever abides in me and I in him, he it is that bears much fruit, for apart from me you can do nothing. If anyone does not abide in me he is thrown away like a branch and withers; and the branches are gathered, thrown into the *fire*, and burned (John 15:1–6).

In verse 4, Jesus said, "As the branch cannot bear fruit of itself, except it abide in the vine, no more can ye, except you abide in me."

In verse 5, He rephrases it. "Without Me, you can do nothing!"

The word *abide* occurs five times in these six verses. Some versions use the word *remain*. There is a difference between those words. The Greek word can be translated either *abide* or *remain*. But the context definitely demands one and not the other English word. Our English word, *remain*, is static, dead. You can put a book, ring, stone, or other inanimate object down and unless someone else takes it or there is a force powerful enough to move it, that object will remain. That is not what this passage is about. The word *abide* means to exist, to live. God does not expect us to remain in Christ. He expects us to live in Christ and allow Him to live in and through us. Read Galatians 2:20; the word *live* occurs four times. The word *remain* does not exist in that verse. "I have been crucified with Christ. It is no longer I who *live*, but Christ who *lives* in me. And the life I now *live* in the flesh I *live* by faith in the Son of God, who loved me and gave himself for me" (Galatians 2:20).

As we saw before, God the Father is the Farmer who cares for the vine, the trunk of which is the Only Begotten Son of God, the second person of the eternal Trinity who, in His incarnation, added humanity to who He was to that He would live a perfect human life, suffer tremendously, die as the once for all Passover Lamb, and live again, never ceasing to be fully human and fully God. The branches are Christians, believers in God's promise of salvation, indwelt by the Holy Spirit. God the Father desires a return, a profit on his investment, the suffering and death of Jesus Christ, which profit is spiritual fruit in and through His children, because the fruit comes from the branches, from we Christians. God is a good farmer. 1 Corinthians 3:9 tells us that we believers are God's helpers, "For we are God's fellow workers. You are God's [cultivated] field, God's building." The Holy Spirit, by the direction and power of God the Father through Jesus Christ, prepares the way for us, supplying the power-giving grace, first for salvation, and then for doing God's work after salvation. Ephesians 2:10 informs us, "For we are his workmanship, created in Christ Jesus for good works, which God prepared beforehand, that we should walk in them."

How does the vine bring increase? With the combination of nourishment from the prepared soil, water, and sunlight, life-sustaining sap goes from the roots of the vine to the trunk, and through the trunk to the branches. That life-sustaining sap goes on to do what the vine was created to do. It produces flowers, then fruit. If the vine bears enough fruit, it brings the profit that the Farmer is looking for and expecting. In the same way, God, the Master, prepares the heart of a person through grace. By grace, the prepared heart is ready to believe, and God gives the faith to believe. The new believer is planted into the Family of God, in which Jesus Christ is the head, or trunk. Colossians 1:18 tells us, "And he is the head of the body, the church. He is the beginning, the firstborn from the dead, that in everything he might be preeminent." Ephesians 1:22-23 states, "And he put all things under his feet and gave him as head over all things to the church, which is his body, the fullness of him who fills all in all."

As expected, many, even most, of the branches bear fruit. Those branches he purges, trims. We tend to think, "If it is not broken, why fix it!" But that doesn't apply to the vineyard. God, the Farmer, prunes the fruit-bearing branches! Why? God takes away activities, friends, or belongings that interfere with the Christian bearing more fruit. That just doesn't sound fair, does it. The truth of the matter is that we are far more fulfilled and satisfied with our lives when we spend more time in God's work rather than in worldly pleasures.

But some of the branches do not bear fruit. Every branch in Christ that does not bear fruit, what does the God the Father, the Farmer, do? Let's look at the passage a little closer. In John 15:2, the English text says, "Every branch of mine that does not bear fruit he takes away, and every branch that does bear fruit he prunes, that it may bear more fruit."

When we look at passages, we need to forget that verse numbers are there. We look, word by word and verse by verse, at a passage, and see what makes sense. This part says that, if a branch does not bear fruit, God, the Farmer, takes the branch away. But does it make sense, in this passage, and in the context of the whole Bible, that this is really what God is telling us? We need to be careful to keep from being guilty of false interpretation, reading into the Bible what we want to see. But we can use the tools God made available, which is, first, the Complete Word of God, and also the original language texts. The English text tells us that every branch that does not bear fruit, he takes away. Then, a few words later, He next tells us that we are clean, or acceptable to God, through the Word of God, given to us and received by us. Remember that Jesus Christ is the Vine. We who believe are branches. We, who believe, are saved. We have received salvation. We are in the vine. Can we stop being in the vine? No, the Bible does not teach that.

> Who shall separate us from the love of Christ? Shall tribulation, or distress, or persecution, or famine, or nakedness, or danger, or sword? As it is written, "For your sake we are being killed all the day long; we are regarded as sheep to be slaughtered." No, in all these things we are more than conquerors through him who loved us. For I am sure that neither death nor life, nor angels nor rulers, nor things present nor things to come, nor powers, nor height nor depth, nor anything else in all creation, will be able to *separate* us from the love of God in Christ Jesus our Lord" (Rom. 8:35–39; emphasis added).

Nothing or no being will be able to separate us from the love of God in Jesus Christ, our Lord. It is impossible to lose or give up salvation. The text, in verse 39, says, "Nor any other creature." Any other creature includes every creature not mentioned, such as demons, Satan, and even ourselves.

John 15:2 tells us that "every branch of mine that does not bear fruit He *takes away*." This author had always been uncomfortable with those two words, *takes away*, because they just do not fit the text! The book *Secrets of the Vine* by Bruce Wilkenson (Multnoma, Oct. 2001), is a great little book well worth reading. Wilkenson wrote that the Greek word for "taketh away," transliterated *airo*, means to *raise up*. That meaning does fit the text. I did more study.

First of all, John 15:6 tells us the same thing as we see in the English in verse 2, "If anyone does not abide in me he is thrown away like a branch and withers; and the branches are gathered, thrown into the fire and burned." A continuously rebellious Christian is removed from this life early.

Then we can look at the common usage of the word in the Greek culture. In common usage *airo* meant things like "take out the garbage to dispose of it." In that usage, the word would literally mean to *raise up* and then to carry away, or to move after *raising it up*.

Finally, we can look at some other passages using the Greek word *airo* are:

- Matthew 4:6 states that Jesus was on the Mount of Temptation being tempted by Satan, who "said to him, 'If you are the Son of God, throw yourself down, for it is written, He will command his angels concerning you,' and 'On their hands they will *bear you up*, lest you strike your foot against a stone.'"

- Matthew 9:6 states, "'But that you may know that the Son of Man has authority on earth to forgive sins'—he then said to the paralytic—'Rise, *pick up* your bed and go home.'"

- Matthew 16:24 states, "Then Jesus told his disciples, 'If anyone would come after me, let him deny himself and *take up* his cross and follow me.'"

The actual meaning of the Greek word is to "bear up," "take up" or "pick up." In order to throw something away, you first have to lift or pick it up. We have to look at the context in which the word is used. Literally, the passage says, "Every branch in me that does not bear fruit he picks up, or lifts up."

Since the branch is already in the vine, Jesus Christ, the person who is the branch is truly saved. If the person does not bear fruit, will the Farmer, God, just throw the branch away? What does a good farmer do?

Let's look at Luke 13:6–9:

And he told this parable: "A man had a fig tree planted in his vineyard, and he came seeking fruit on it and found none. And he said to the vinedresser, 'Look, for three years now I have come seeking fruit on this fig tree, and I find none. Cut it down. Why should it use up the ground?' And he answered him, 'Sir, let it alone this year also, until I dig around it and put on manure. Then if it should bear fruit next year, well and good; but if not, you can cut it down.'"

The caretaker did not want to cut down the fig tree immediately and cast it out or burn it. First he cared for it in a loving way, giving more attention to that tree than to the others. Only after a prolonged time period and after much effort would he be willing to cast it away.

God is the same way with His people. He is long suffering and patient. He will continue to work with the His people. But not indefinitely, as we saw in verse 6.

Back to John 15. The branch is in Christ. The branch does not bear fruit. Why?

The branch may be laying in the dirt. Grape branches must be in the air and sunlight to produce fruit and needs to be taken up out of the dirt and washed off. The branch may be underneath other branches. It does not get sunlight, so it cannot produce fruit. The Farmer needs to lift the branch out of the shade and put it where it will get sunlight, tying it in place, if need be, to train it to stay in the sunlight. There are great spiritual applications here, being corrupted by the dirt of sin, being out of dynamic fellowship in the Sonlight of the Son of God.

When God takes us out of the dirt of worldliness, it is seldom comfortable. We tend to fight God. That is why He ties us in place. Only after much care and patience will he cast the branch away; the sinner will die. For the branch, being in the dirt and / or out of the sunlight is not in the best position to bear fruit. The Farmer repositions it to get more sunlight and stay clean. He lifts it up out of the dirt. And he generally has to train it to stay in place to be in a position that it can bear fruit! The same is true for the Christian who does not bear fruit. Sometimes pain is involved!

What about the branch that bears fruit? The farmer prunes it. A good healthy vine is not a real leafy, showy plant. It does not have all that many leaves, and it does not have all that many small branches to steal away that life-giving sap. Those are cut away so the sap goes toward making more fruit. The branches it does have are big and beefy, capable of having a lot of the life-giving sap flow into and through it. For the sole purpose of the branch is to bear fruit. The parable of the sower says up to a hundredfold (Luke 8:8).

Have you ever wondered why God did not just take us to heaven when we accepted Him as Savior? It is because He has work for us to do—to bear fruit for Him and to His glory!

I think each of us agrees that we are not bearing fruit as God expects.

"For we are his workmanship, created in Christ Jesus unto good works, which God hath before ordained that we should walk in them." Pray for God's help in submitting to Him.

10

A Study of the Vine and Its Branches: Part 2

In the last chapter, we looked at fruit bearing plants as a picture of God's people, and what God expects out of those plants, or out of His people. We will start with another parable.

> "A man had a fig tree planted in his vineyard, and he came seeking fruit on it and found none. And he said to the vinedresser, 'Look, for three years now I have come seeking fruit on this fig tree, and I find none. Cut it down. Why should it use up the ground?' And he answered him, 'Sir, let it alone this year also, until I dig around it and put on manure. Then if it should bear fruit next year, well and good; but if not, you can cut it down'" (Luke 13:6-9).

The caretaker did not immediately cut off the tree and cast it out or burn it. First he cared for it in a loving way, giving more attention to that tree than to the others. Only after a prolonged time period and after much effort would he cast it away. God is long suffering. He is not impatient. He will continue to work with the plant. But not indefinitely.

We looked at the parable of the Soils. According to parable of the Sower and Soils in Luke 8, the Sower is the Holy Spirit who spreads the Seed, which is the Gospel, to the four different types of Soil, representing four different types of acceptance of the Gospel, the hardened path which totally rejects the Gospel, the shallow soil which considers acceptance, but soon rejects it, the soil in which weed seeds flourish, which considers thee Gospel and gives assent with the head but does not with the heart, and the soil which was worked adequately by the farmer to not only to receive the Gospel, but to flourish and produce a profit.

> A sower went out to sow his seed. And as he sowed, some fell along the path and was trampled underfoot, and the birds of the air devoured it. And some fell on the rock, and as it grew up, it withered away, because it had no moisture. And some fell among thorns, and the thorns grew up with it and choked it. And some fell into good soil and grew and yielded a hundredfold." As he said these things, he called out, "He who has ears to hear, let him hear (Luke 8:5–8a).

What does God really desire, or expect, from those whom are represented by the four different soils? He desires much increase even to hundredfold. Is it possible for God to mercifully and graciously give salvation to the three types of reception to the Gospel which had rejected it that salvation?

Now, let's continue to look at John 15, the True Vine.

> I am the true vine, and my Father is the vinedresser. Every branch of mine that does not bear fruit he takes away, and every branch that does bear fruit he prunes, that it may bear more fruit. Already you are clean because of the word that I have spoken to you. Abide in me, and I in you. As the branch cannot bear fruit by itself, unless it abides in the vine, neither can you, unless you abide in

me. I am the vine; you are the branches. Whoever abides in me and I in him, he it is that bears much fruit, for apart from me you can do nothing. If anyone does not abide in me he is thrown away like a branch and withers; and the branches are gathered, thrown into the fire, and burned. If you abide in me, and my words abide in you, ask whatever you wish, and it will be done for you. By this my Father is glorified, that you bear much fruit and so prove to be my disciples (John 15:1–8).

God the Father is the vine dresser who cares for the vine. Jesus Christ is the vine. He is the trunk and passes on the nourishment, energy, and direction from the Father to the branches. Christians are the branches of the vine which must receive their sustenance and energy from the trunk, Jesus Christ, to bear fruit. What is the fruit that God desires from the vineyard?

- Spiritual growth, maturity, and wisdom, all through much time spent in the Word of God and prayer, produced by the Holy Spirit, who works through the Word and prayer.

- Thoughts and actions that are based upon obedience to God and given in His Word (Eph. 2:10; Rom. 12:1–3).

- Witnessing, testimonies, and sharing the Gospel with others, leading them to salvation in Jesus Christ when they don't ignore or reject the work of the Holy Spirit

Every branch that does not bear fruit the Father does what to? I reiterate that the Greek word translated as "*takes away*" is from the Greek word which means to "take up." None of the major English versions give the best meaning for this verse. In verse 2, the branch that does not bear fruit is *lifted up* out of the dirt where it is dirty and out of the necessary *sunlight*. In the dirt, the branch will rot and be spoiled with mud. Out of the sunlight, the branch will not be able to gain the energy to bear fruit. The vine dresser, who is the Father, lifts the dirty, filthy, anemic branch out of the dirt and into the sunlight. He cleans it off and gives it support so it will be in the sun where it will bear fruit. It cannot bear fruit in the dirt or out of the sunlight.

It can bear fruit in the sun. The branch in the dirt is figurative of the Christian who is living in *sin*. That Christian is still connected to the vine, Jesus Christ, but rejects the light of Christ and therefore does not produce fruit. That Christian does not necessarily want to come out of the dirt. He or she may be happy there. But God expects fruit from that branch because it is connected, through salvation, to Jesus Christ. The Father could cut the branch off of the vine and give physical death. In fact, He will cut off that branch if it will not, after time, come out of the dirt, out of sin. But instead, the Father's goal is to give *life* so that the branch is more than willing to do what it is supposed to do, produce *fruit* by God's grace. He lifts the Christian out of the fruitless life of living outside of grace and places him where he will be in fellowship with Jesus Christ by God's grace. This process of change is not generally easy. It does involve *chastening*, because the person is in sin. It will involve cleansing, even scrubbing. It will involve cutting the rotten and dead parts of the leaves and branch away. It will be painful. But the branch will be given the chance to bear fruit. Chastening is not punishment so much as it is attention getting; God will do whatever it takes to get our attention when we are living in sin. God chastens us as parents chasten their children (Hebrews 12:6). He starts with a reproof (rebuke). If that does not work, He uses stronger language to get our attention and maybe removing possessions or people who keep us in sin, even sickness in ourselves or even our loved ones, or even the death of a loved one; He will do whatever it takes to get our attention. He starts gently but uses harsher means when the gentle reproof does not work.

If a Christian will not respond to chastening, God will, at some point, take that Christian *out* of the *world* because he or she is not *bearing fruit*:

- Verse 6 states, "If anyone does not abide in me he is thrown away like a branch and withers; and the branches are gathered, thrown into the fire, and burned."

- First Corinthians 11:30 states, "That is why many of you are weak and ill, and some have died."

- First John 5:16 states, "…There is a sin unto death…"

What is the only way to get out of the dirt? God the Father chastises us to get us out of the dirt. But the choice to stay out of the dirt has to be our own, by the grace (power) of God. That choice only comes one way.

Matthew 3:7–8 states, "But when he saw many of the Pharisees and Sadducees coming for baptism, he said to them, "You brood of vipers! Who warned you to flee from the wrath to come? Bear fruit in keeping with repentance."

Then comes 1 John 1:9, which has to happen before the Christian can enter again into that relationship with Jesus Christ (there is no loss of salvation because of sin, but there is loss of relationship). There must be repentance, then asking forgiveness. The repentance has to involve humility before Jesus Christ in recognizing that He is right and that He is Lord and that we were wrong and are only servants. We are either obedient servants bearing fruit, or we are disobedient servants who don't bear fruit because of *sin*.

In the second part of 1 John 15:2, we see that "…every branch that does bear fruit he prunes, that it may bear more fruit." The branch that bears fruit is in fellowship with Jesus Christ and is an obedient servant. We are bearing fruit in our lives in Christ. But Jesus Christ, who made us and saved us, knows us better than we know ourselves. God has a pathway already mapped out for each of us to bear more fruit. We have not yet found that pathway, even though we are obedient and bearing fruit. So, as a herding dog will do with sheep, God guides us to the path He set for us. In that guidance, He puts roadblocks of some kind or another in our way to direct us to where He wants us to be. We don't like those roadblocks. We want to keep going in the direction that we have been going. But God knows best. Sometimes the roadblocks set us back in different ways. Relationships are severed, we have financial problems, and we may have to relocate. Something happens to change our way. This is not chastening because we are obedient. This is pruning or purging. The Greek word for "prune" means to clean. A primary use for the word is to "prune."

In the pruning, unnecessary things are being cut out of our lives. God knows that we are more capable of bearing more fruit by going down another path. God directs us that way through purging, or pruning, us. We may be compromised with the world through possessions. God removes those possessions through purging so we may not be compromised. We may have friends that cause us to be less than completely dedicated to God. God will cause us to know that we have to sever those relationships. God puts us down another path than the path we have been on. He knows best. When we are pruned, or purified, we will bear more fruit. On the grape vine, too many branches and leaves take up too much energy, so the energy is not being used to bear fruit. For us, the unnecessary things are things that keep us from bearing more fruit. We think that we are doing very good in bearing the fruit that we do bear. But our understanding is incomplete. Proverbs 3:5–6 states, "Trust in the LORD with all your heart, and do not lean on your own understanding. In all your ways acknowledge him, and he will make straight your paths." God, the vine dresser, cuts off these extra leaves and the new buds and / or twigs from the branch because He wants the energy to be focused in another way. He knows best. This pruning is purging. It is making us more productive.

John 15:3 states, "Already you are clean because of the word that I have spoken to you." We are clean, pruned, through hearing God's Word. The word pruned in verse 2 and clean in verse 3 are related. "Prune" comes from "clean." The word *clean* is actually a reference to the Levitical cleanness. It refers to the purity that God demands before one comes into His presence to serve Him. We are clean through God's Word. But this verse does not stand alone. N verse 2, we are chastened, and then we are pruned. Then comes verse 3. After we are chastened and repent from sin and ask forgiveness, and after we are pruned from things that keep us from being totally dedicated to Christ, we are clean. This happens from the Holy Spirit working through the Word of God.

Let's recap verses 1 thru 3.

Verse 1 establishes the parameters. God the Father is the vine dresser. God the Son is the Vine. We are the branches. As branches in the vine, we are saved. But we are also responsible to bear fruit for the Father by the Son through power the Holy Spirit.

Verse 2 shows sin and shows life direction and how God the Father handles these. God chastens the sinful and prunes out anything that compromises us in the obedient Christian.

Verse 3 says that, now, after we have been chastised and while we are being pruned, we are clean. Prune, in verse 2, is in simple present tense, meaning that it is currently happening. We have been rebuked by the Word, we have repented and asked forgiveness, and then are being set on God's path for us. We are made *clean* by God's grace in the sense that we are acceptable in God's presence and to do His work, like the Levites were expected to clean themselves before coming to the temple to serve Him.

Another passage in the New Testament that talks about the Word of God being the instrument to make us usable for God's work. Second Timothy 3:16–17 states, "All Scripture is breathed out by God and profitable for teaching, for reproof, for correction, and for training in righteousness, that the man of God may be complete, equipped for every good work."

In John 15:4, Jesus says to abide in Him. This is in the active voice, meaning that it is our choice to abide in Him, which is only possible by His grace. He will not make us do it. When we abide in Him, He abides in us. What does it mean to abide? Let's look at the meaning of the whole context here.

Some English versions use the word *remain* in place of *abide*. The Greek word can be used either way. But, looking at the context, *remain* does not fit. We can "remain" in Christ with the idea that we rest in Him, with no activity (*remain* is passive). There is nothing wrong with the idea of resting in Christ. But that is not what John is saying in this chapter. John is talking about a relationship. We are to abide in Christ. The idea is to remain connected in a vibrant, active relationship with Him, empowered by God's grace.

- The *People's New Testament Commentary* says, "The idea is, Abide in me that I may abide in you. Christ abiding in us is dependent on our abiding in him." (*People's New Testament Commentary*, Power Bible CD 4.2 copyright 2004 by Online Publishing, Inc, P.O. Box 21, Bronson, MI 49028, note on John 15:4)

- Albert Barnes paraphrases it, "Remain united to me by a *living* faith. Live a life of dependence on me, and obey my doctrines, imitate my example, and constantly exercise faith in me…if you remain attached to me, I will remain with you, and will teach, guide, and comfort you." (Barnes Notes, Online Bible Edition Ver. 2.10.00.03, 6/25/2016, copyright 1995–2016 by Online Bible Foundation, Carluke, Lanarkshire, Scotland, M/8 4PZ, note on John 15:4)

- The *Family Bible Notes* states, "The union between Christ and his disciples is mutual. They abide in him by faith, love, and obedience. He abides in them through the Holy Spirit, as the source of their spiritual life, light, and strength." (*Family New Testament Notes*, Online Bible Foundation, Ibid, Note on John 15:4)

- Robertson's NT Word Pictures says, "The only way to continue 'clean' (pruned) and to bear fruit is to maintain vital spiritual connexion with Christ (the vine)." (Robertson's NT Word Pictures, Online Bible Foundation, Ibid, Note on John 15:4)

Jesus Christ said that, if we abide in Him (maintain a vital relationship with Him), He will abide in us (reciprocate that relationship as He works in and through us). The meaning is active, meaning *to live* (John 10:10) or *to dwell*. The English Standard and King James Versions put it well using the word *abide*.

This is all about a vital, personal relationship with Jesus Christ. We must have no unforgiven sin between us and God (1 John 1:9). We must be willing to go where He leads.

- Galatians 2:20 states, "I have been crucified with Christ. It is no longer I who live, but Christ who lives in me. And the life I now live in the flesh I live by faith in the Son of God, who loved me and gave himself for me."

- Second Corinthians 4:6–11 states, "For God, who said, 'Let light shine out of darkness,' has shone in our hearts to give the light of the knowledge of the glory of God in the face of Jesus Christ. But we have this treasure in jars of clay, to show that the surpassing power belongs to God and not to us. We are afflicted in every way, but not crushed; perplexed, but not driven to despair; persecuted, but not forsaken; struck down, but not destroyed; always carrying in the body the death of Jesus, so that the life of Jesus may also be manifested in our bodies. For we who live are always being given over to death for Jesus' sake, so that the life of Jesus also may be manifested in our mortal flesh."

We must abide in Him, meaning that we must continuously work on our relationship with Him by spending personal daily time with Him in His Word and in prayer. When we do that, He lives in and through us. He not only remains in us, but He sets up house and works in us. When that happens, we bear fruit. The rest of verse 4 states that "as the branch cannot bear fruit of itself, except it abide in the vine; no more can ye, except ye abide in me."

A close personal relationship with Christ equals bearing much fruit. That does not mean we won't have problems. Pruning is generally about problems. If we don't have problems, we may not be saved (Hebrews 12:6 tells us, "For the Lord disciplines the one he loves, and chastises every son whom he receives." An equation is, problems+God's Word+submission=God's wisdom. Pruning is something that comes often and happens in some way or another. Pruning brings wisdom. Pruning is in simple present tense, meaning that it is always present. Verse 5 states, "I am the vine; you are the branches. Whoever abides in me and I in him, he it is that bears much fruit, for apart from me you can do nothing."

So John 15, about the Vine, is about abiding in Christ to bear fruit. This is specifically about a thriving personal relationship with Jesus Christ. This relationship does not come from living in doctrine or accurate interpretation of the Bible. Knowledge comes from that and is very important; doctrine and accurate interpretation are the foundation of the Christian life. The close personal relationship, which is living the Christian life, comes from personal communication from God through His Word, and our personal communication to Him through prayer. This close personal relationship comes only from daily time spent with Him without hindrance.

Does the parable of the Talents have something to do with what we are discussing in the Vine?

Parable of the Talents

"For it [the kingdom of God] will be like a man going on a journey, who called his servants and entrusted to them his property. To one he gave five talents, to another two, to another one, to each according to his ability. Then he went away. He who had received the five talents went at once and traded with them, and he made five talents more. So also he who had the two talents made two talents more. But he who had received the one talent went and dug in the ground and hid his master's money. Now after a long time the master of those servants came and settled accounts with them. And he who had received the five talents came forward, bringing five talents more, saying, 'Master, you delivered to me five talents; here I have made five talents more.' His master said to him, 'Well done, good and faithful servant. You have been faithful over a little; I will set you over much. Enter into the joy of your master.' And he also who had the two talents came forward, saying, 'Master, you delivered to me two talents; here I have made two talents more.' His master said to him, 'Well done, good and faithful servant. You have been faithful over a little; I will set you over much. Enter into the joy of your master.' He also who had received the one talent came forward, saying, 'Master, I knew you to be a hard man, reaping where you did not sow, and gathering where you scattered no seed, so I was afraid, and I went and hid your talent in the ground. Here you have what is yours.' But his master answered him, 'You wicked and slothful servant! You knew that I reap where I have not sowed and gather where I scattered no seed? Then you ought to have invested my money with the bankers, and at my coming I should have received what was my own with interest. So take the talent from him and give it to him who has the ten talents. For to everyone who has will more be given, and he will have an abundance. But from the one who has not, even what he has will be taken away. And cast the worthless servant into the outer darkness. In that place there will be weeping and gnashing of teeth.' (Matt. 25:14–30)

- God does not expect the same amount of fruit out of every Christian. But He does expect a good return on His investment, which is the humanity, suffering and death of His Son.

- God does not play favorites. He said the same thing to the person with the two talents as He did the person with five talents. "Well done, good and faithful servant. You have been faithful over a little; I will set you over much. Enter into the joy of your master."

- The closer the relationship with Jesus Christ, the greater the return from the Master. It is in our best interest to bear much fruit. It not only pleases God, it will be pleasing and satisfying to us.

- When we look at the third servant, did he sin? What was his attitude? During the long time that the Master was away, his attitude did not change. He was actually in a subtle rebellion against God. He was in sin. He gained no rewards because he bore no fruit. He is chastised by being cast into the outer darkness, which, in this case, is separation from fellowship with

11

A Study of the Vine and Its Branches: Part 3

In the first and second chapters, we saw that God wants and expects us to bear fruit. He disciplines those who are in unforgiven sin. It is not possible to bear fruit for God when we have unforgiven sin between Him and us.

In this chapter, I would like to cover the following subjects.

- What does it mean to bear fruit?
- How does God work with us to bear fruit?
    - More Fruit.
    - Much Fruit.
- What is the secret to bearing Much Fruit?

What Does It Mean to Bear Fruit?

> Therefore be imitators of God, as beloved children. And
> walk in love, as Christ loved us and gave himself up for

us, a fragrant offering and sacrifice to God. But sexual immorality and all impurity or covetousness must not even be named among you, as is proper among saints. Let there be no filthiness nor foolish talk nor crude joking, which are out of place, but instead let there be thanksgiving. For you may be sure of this, that everyone who is sexually immoral or impure, or who is covetous (that is, an idolater), has no inheritance in the kingdom of Christ and God. Let no one deceive you with empty words, for because of these things the wrath of God comes upon the sons of disobedience. Therefore do not become partners with them; for at one time you were darkness, but now you are light in the Lord. Walk as children of light (for the fruit of light is found in all that is good and right and true), and try to discern what is pleasing to the Lord. Take no part in the unfruitful works of darkness, but instead expose them. For it is shameful even to speak of the things that they do in secret. But when anything is exposed by the light, it becomes visible, for anything that becomes visible is light. Therefore it says, "Awake, O sleeper, and arise from the dead, and Christ will shine on you." Look carefully then how you walk, not as unwise but as wise, making the best use of the time, because the days are evil. Therefore do not be foolish, but understand what the will of the Lord is. And do not get drunk with wine, for that is debauchery, but be filled with the Spirit, addressing one another in psalms and hymns and spiritual songs, singing and making melody to the Lord with all your heart, giving thanks always and for everything to God the Father in the name of our Lord Jesus Christ, submitting to one another out of reverence for Christ (Ephesians 5:1–21).

This whole passage is about bearing fruit.

- Verse 1 – Be Followers of God
- Verse 2 – Walk in Love (*agape*)

- Verse 3 – "sexual immorality and all impurity or covetousness must not even be named among you, as is proper among saints."

- Verse 4 – Let there be no filthiness nor foolish talk nor crude joking, which are out of place, but instead let there be thanksgiving.

- Verse 5–7 – Do not be guilty of immoral action or words and do not fellowship with those who do.

- Verse 8 – Walk in Light, for we are children of light.

- Verse 9–10 – The Fruit of the Spirit is in all goodness and righteousness and truth, proving what is acceptable unto the Lord.

- Verse 11–12 – Have nothing to do with unfruitful works of spiritual darkness for they are shameful. Rather, reprove them.

- Verse 13–14 – Reprove the darkness of unrighteousness by exposing it to the Light of Christ's righteousness. Christ shall give us the Light through His Word and the Holy Spirit.

- Verse 15–17 – Walk carefully in Christ's wisdom, using time wisely that the Lord's will and work be done in His time.

- Verse 18 – As an alcoholic is controlled by the drink, be controlled by the Holy Spirit by being filled up with Him.

- Verse 19 – Praise God with godly music and song, both in fellowship of the saints and in our heart.

- Verse 20 – Give thanks for all things, because God is in control.

- Verse 21 – Submit to one another in the example of Jesus Christ, and according to His Word.

Galatians 5:22–25 is another passage on fruit of the Spirit: "But the fruit of the Spirit is love, joy, peace, patience, kindness, goodness, faithfulness, gentleness, self-control; against such things there is no law. And those who belong to Christ Jesus have crucified the flesh with its passions and desires. If we live by the Spirit, let us also walk by the Spirit."

Living in the Spirit and *Walking* in the Spirit *is* bearing fruit internally.

Another way of looking at bearing fruit is given in 1 Corinthians 3:11–15:

> For no one can lay a foundation other than that which is laid, which is Jesus Christ. Now if anyone builds on the foundation with gold, silver, precious stones, wood, hay, straw— each one's work will become manifest, for the Day will disclose it, because it will be revealed by fire, and the fire will test what sort of work each one has done. If the work that anyone has built on the foundation survives [fruit is borne], he will receive a reward. If anyone's work is burned up, he will suffer loss, though he himself will be saved, but only as through fire [there is no fruit borne].

So, looking at all these passages we find that Anything done in the Name of the Lord and by His grace is fruit of the Spirit. In 2 Corinthians 5:10, we find that, at the Bema seat, anything we are rewarded for is for the fruit of the Spirit, "For we must all appear before the judgment seat of Christ; that every one may receive the things done in his body, according to that he hath done, whether it be good or bad." This is bearing fruit externally. So what is bearing fruit? Bearing fruit is being controlled by the Holy Spirit in obedience to Jesus Christ.

HOW DOES GOD WORK WITH US TO BEAR MORE FRUIT?

As we had stated from John 15:2, when we are in unforgiven sin, we cannot bear fruit. The Holy Spirit cannot work through us. God wants fruit from us; He wants a profit. That can only accomplished when we allow the Holy Spirit to control us and guide us (grace instead of free will). God's way is hindered when we are in unforgiven sin. So we are disciplined to get our attention and to steer us in the right direction so that we can bear fruit.

God lifts the fallen branches out of the dirt and cleans them off. He ties the branches in the sunlight so that they may bear fruit.

HOW MUCH FRUIT?

When Christians are bearing some fruit, God takes away some of the possessions or habits they have so they can focus their attention on things of God. That is pruning. Then the Christians are able bear *more* fruit. The branch is trimmed of anything that keeps it from bearing lots of fruit. God talks with us through His Word, through circumstances and through friends and acquaintances. We graduate from *some fruit* to *more fruit*.

But there is another level of bearing fruit. It is that extra special close relationship (father-child), or very close fellowship that we can have on a superior level with Jesus Christ.

MUCH FRUIT

When Christians bear more fruit, God gives added direction by causing road blocks or detours in each individual Christian's life. God gives to us unexpected direction when He is leading us to bear *even more* fruit. He has a special, individual path for us in which we will bear *much* fruit. This is *individual* direction rather than *flock* direction. He wants each of us to be the best that we can be. He knows that we cannot find this on our own without special leadership, because our own skills and talents will not lead us there. This giving of direction is also pruning. This is like placing the branch in just the right position so that it gets the most sunlight and trimming each particular branch in the best way possible for it to bear lots of good, delicious fruit. It is individual guidance given to those who are obedient and seeking God.

This is that level discussed in Colossians 1:9–11; 3:10 and 2 Peter 1:2–4.

- Colossians 1:9–11 states, "And so, from the day we heard, we have not ceased to pray for you, asking that you may be filled with the knowledge of his will in all spiritual wisdom and understanding, so as to walk in a manner worthy of the Lord, fully pleasing to him, bearing fruit in every good work and increasing in the knowledge of God; being strengthened with all power, according to his glorious might, for all endurance and patience with joy,"

- Colossians 3:10 states, "and have put on the new self, which is being renewed in knowledge after the image of its creator." The word *knowledge*, here, is the intensified Greek word for knowledge because of the *mature* relationship with our Lord.

- Second Peter 1:2–4 states, "May grace and peace be multiplied to you in the [intensified] knowledge of God and of Jesus our Lord. His divine power has granted to us all things that pertain to life and godliness, through the [intensified] knowledge of him who called us to his own glory and excellence, by which he has granted to us his precious and very great promises, so that through them you may become partakers of the divine nature, having escaped from the corruption that is in the world because of sinful desire."

These verses are talking about bearing much fruit.

WHAT IS THE SECRET TO BEARING MUCH FRUIT?

To receive this individual guidance to *much fruit*, we need a certain attitude.

And the LORD appeared to him by the oaks of Mamre, as he sat at the door of his tent in the heat of the day. He lifted up his eyes and looked, and behold, three men were standing in front of him. When he saw them, he ran from the tent door to meet them and bowed himself to the earth and said, "O Lord, if I have found favor in your sight, do not pass by your servant" (Genesis 18:1–3).

Some commentaries and teachers say that Abraham, following the custom of the middle east courteousness, sat in his tent door waiting for whoever might be coming along to feed the traveler and give him rest. That is not why Abraham was waiting.

Look at the chapter before, Genesis 17:1–6:

When Abram was ninety-nine years old the LORD appeared to Abram and said to him, "I am God Almighty; walk before me, and be blameless, that I may make my covenant between me and you, and may multiply you greatly." Then Abram fell on his face. And God said to him, "Behold, my covenant is with you, and you shall be the father of a multitude of nations. No longer shall your name be called Abram, but your name shall be Abraham, for I have made you the father of a multitude of nations. I will make you exceedingly fruitful, and I will make you into nations, and kings shall come from you.

God told Abraham more of the covenant that God was divulging over time. Then God gave Abraham the mind-blowing promise.

And God said to Abraham, "As for Sarai your wife, you shall not call her name Sarai, but Sarah shall be her name. I will bless her, and moreover, I will give you a son by her. I will bless her, and she shall become nations; kings of peoples shall come from her. But I will establish my covenant with Isaac, whom Sarah shall bear to you at this time next year [the transliterated Hebrew says *at the set time in another year*]." When he had finished talking with him, God went up from Abraham" (Genesis 17:15–16, 21–22).

Abraham, knowing the time for a woman from conception to birth, was waiting for a particular person who we know was a pre-incarnate appearance of Jesus Christ who had told Abraham that, at a time set by God, in another year, possibly the following year, Sarah would bear a the promised son. Abraham believed in miracles because God promised it. Abraham was waiting for God to come and make that miracle happen.

That must be our attitude when we want to bear much fruit. Like Abraham, we must expectantly look for our meeting with the Lord. This should be our attitude every morning when we sit to be with Him in our daily devotions. Expect Him to talk to us. Desire to be with Him. He has promised, and He will make it come to pass. He will, if we let Him, make us to be the person He created us to be. We will then bear much fruit. Psalms 119:130–131 states, "The unfolding of your words gives light; it imparts understanding to the simple. I open my mouth and pant, because I long for your commandments."

God wants to fellowship with us; He wants to deal with us in a very close and personal way. As we mature in our relationship with Him, He communicates with us through His Word in a different way than before. He will lead, direct, and equip us to be the person He created us to be and to do what He preordained for us to do.

It is important to understand the importance of accurate interpretation of the Bible. The accurate interpretation of the Bible, along with sound doctrine, is foundational to the Christian life. It gives us our boundaries in all ways of life, as well as the Gospel and prophecy. It is of tremendous importance to us. It is the *Logos* (John 1:1), the complete, intelligible, communicated Word from God to us.

Sound doctrine is obtained from accurate interpretation of the Bible. There are also principles that we receive from the Bible. These principles may or may not be explicitly stated whereas doctrine is always true. A principle is generally true, but not always. Principles apply to everyone. Proverbs is full of principles. An example of a proverb that is a principle but not doctrine is Proverbs 22:6, "Train up a child in the way he should go; even when he is old he will not depart from it." We can do our very best to train a child. But the child still has freewill and may choose his or her own way in spite of our best efforts.

Other principles are taken from what passages seem to say and can be supported by other biblical passages. An example is that God has ordained the man of the family to earn a living and the woman to keep the house. That does not mean that the man does not help with the house and that the woman cannot help earn the living. But the responsibilities for each is given. We get that principle from Genesis 3:16–19, Proverbs 31: 10–31, Titus 2:3–5, as well as other passages.

Another principle is that, if we let Him, God will introduce a single (unmarried) person to his or her mate. We see this through several doctrines or principles.

- God purchased us. He owns us. He is all knowing. He knows best. Who is better prepared to choose our mate than Him?

- Dating is inviting big trouble. A young person is to be under the guidance and leadership of his or her parents until the time of marriage. That young person's love emotions involving another person of the opposite sex belong to his or her future mate. Any love emotions going to another person are actually stolen from the future mate that God intended. It is innocence lost.

- Broken relationships with others always cause damage that will interfere with the pure relation ship that a man and wife should have.

- God said He is in charge in this area. Proverbs 19:14 (emphasis added) states, "House and wealth are inherited from fathers, *but a prudent wife is from the LORD.*"

- Singles need to focus on things other than the opposite sex. First Corinthians 7:33–35 states, "But the married man is anxious about worldly things, how to please his wife, and his interests are divided. And the unmarried or betrothed woman is anxious about the things of the Lord, how to be holy in body and spirit... I say this for your own benefit, not to lay any restraint upon you, but to promote good order and *to secure your undivided devotion to the Lord.*"

Principles do not have to follow accurate interpretation of the Word of God, but they will never go against accurate interpretation. Paul used an Old Testament example of feeding an ox to discuss paying pastors.

First Corinthians 9:8-9 and First Timothy 5:17–18 states, "Let the elders who rule well be considered worthy of double honor, especially those who labor in preaching and teaching. For the Scripture says, 'You shall not muzzle an ox when it treads out the grain,' and, 'The laborer deserves his wages.'" In that passage, Paul quoted of Deuteronomy 25:4: "'You shall not muzzle an ox when it is treading out the grain'." The Holy Spirit directed Paul to use this verse about treating animals fairly to teach a lesson about paying pastors.

So principles apply to all people. Violation of principles is not a sin. Principles are not laws. Principles guide a person or group of people to greater success and less loss, but they are not laws.

RHEMA OR PERSONAL COMMUNICATION FROM GOD

There is another type of communication from God through His Word that can very personal. Where the *logos* is the complete Word of God (John 1:1), a *rhema* is an understandable, logical portion of the Word of God (Ephesians 6:17b). It is can be doctrine but does not have to be doctrine. It is can be a general principle but does not have to be. It is personal communication from God. This is one of the ways that we can grow to be in a mature relationship with Jesus Christ.

There are many use of a *rhema* in the Bible: Some examples are:

- Jesus was under arrest. Peter had just denied Jesus 3 times, and the cock crowed. Matthew 26:75 states, "And Peter remembered the saying [rhema] of Jesus, 'Before the rooster crows, you will deny me three times'. And he went out and wept bitterly."

- The angel Gabriel came to Mary to tell her that she was chosen to be the mother of God. Luke 1 :38 states, "And Mary said, 'Behold, I am the servant of the Lord; let it be to me according to you' word [rhema].' And the angel departed from her."

- John 15:7 states, "If you abide in me, and my words [rhema] abide in you, ask whatever you wish, and it will be done unto you." God will do what we ask because His *rhema* is abiding in us, and we are asking for what He wants us to request.

These words, *rhemas*, are the words of the Bible, the Word of God. But they are personal words to bring salvation, to bring power to bear fruit, to do God's will.

W. E. Vine, in his *An Expository Dictionary of Biblical Words*, writes about the difference between *logos* and *rhema*. "The significance of *rhema* (as distinct from *logos*) is exemplified in the injunction to take 'the sword of the Spirit, which is the word of God,' Ephesians 6:17; here the reference is not to the whole Bible as such, but to the individual scripture which the Spirit brings to our remembrance for use in time of need, a prerequisite being the regular storing of the mind with Scripture" (Thomas Nelson Publishers, Camden, NY, 1985 pg. 683).

Therefore take up the whole armor of God, that you may be able to withstand in the evil day, and having done all, to stand firm... Take the helmet of salvation, and the sword of the Spirit, which is the word [rhema] of God. (Ephesians 6:13 and17)

A *rhema* is like a personal communication to a person or group of people. Memory verses are *rhemas*. God can bring them to mind when He wants to. He talks to us that way, encourages us, and leads or directs us. It is the same with morning devotions. God often uses a *rhema* for a personal communication to us to guide and direct us in bearing fruit at a particular time, or as personal direction. *Rhemas never* go against God's Word. He never denies Himself.

I knew a Christian couple that I won't identify, either in time or place. He worked as a salesman at a parts supply business. She worked for me in a manufacturing plant. They both thought they had received a personal call from the Lord to go into full-time ministry. He quit work to go to a local Baptist Bible college. She quit work to go to another Baptist Bible college in another state. Because they were both *directed (?)* by God to do these things, they ended up working against each other. It caused a divorce. One or both of these *rhemas* was misunderstood or completely wrong! Or to put it another way, one or both of these *rhemas* were from freewill rather than from the grace of God's will. A *rhema* can never be used to lead against God's Word.

What is our attitude in our walking with out Lord? Are we willing to wait upon Him, learn from His Word while we spend much time with Him, expect His leading, and test what we think He has communicated with God's Word? Or are we going to let our own free will and desires lead us? Are we going to bear *much* fruit for Him?

12

SPIRITUAL GROWTH—
POTENTIAL PHASES

The spiritual life of a Christian starts at salvation. Most Christians understand that (John 1:12-13, "But to all who did receive him, who believed in his name, he gave the right to become children of God,"). There are no grandchildren in Christianity. Every member of the Christian community, the body of Christ, is in the body of Christ because of a *personal* decision to accept Jesus Christ as Savior.

Confusion comes from the question, "How does that experience of salvation come to be in a Christian's life?" Most will say that they are saved because they, of their own freewill, accepted Jesus Christ as Savior. Those of us that read the Bible regularly know that we are saved by grace through faith (Ephesians 2:8a, "For by grace are ye saved through faith;..."). But, in our self-centered pride, we still want to believe that we have accepted Jesus Christ as Savior by our own freewill decision, which is impossible, according to the Bible (Ephesians 2:8b, "...and that not of yourselves: it is the gift of God:"). Actually, salvation is not in the active tense to the person; it is very passive. The work of salvation is all from God by God's love and faith, mercy and grace, the work of the Holy Spirit and the Word of God.

It is the belief of this author, based upon years of study, that the Bible's use of the word *grace*, used to describe a work of God, is very much misunderstood. That is what chapter 2 of this book is about. Lewis Sperry Chafer's *Systematic Theology* for Ephesians 2:8–10 (Copyright 1948 and 1976 by Dallas Theological Seminary, Kregel Publications, division of Kregel, Inc., P.O. Box 2607, Grand Rapids, Michigan, 49501). Volume 3, page 6 states:

> No greater fact regarding divine salvation can be declared than is asserted in Jonah 2:9 (RV), 'Salvation belongeth unto Jehovah.' The truth that salvation is of Jehovah is sustained both by revelation and by reason. As for revelation, it is the testimony of the Scriptures, without exception, that every feature of man's salvation from its inception to the final perfection in heaven is a work of God for man, and not a work of man for God. As for reason, there need be but a moment's consideration of the supernatural character of every step in this great achievement to discover that man could contribute nothing whatsoever to its realization. That every step is by faith is a necessity since man, having no power to effect a supernatural result, must be cast back in faith upon Another who is able.

At the point of salvation, we become acceptable to God because of the grace and faith that He gave us. We had not been acceptable to God because of the previous sin of not believing in Him. Through the Holy Spirit, who becomes part of the believer's life, we are strongly urged to talk to God, inaudibly in our mind or audibly to ask God for that repentance that He had already worked in us and to give thanks for salvation. Then we are strongly urged to share with others the testimony of a child of God (Romans 10:9–10). Why? Because self-centered freewill has been overcome by grace at that moment of salvation! We have become a new creation. Second Corinthians 5:17 states, "Therefore, if anyone is in Christ, he is a new creation. The old has passed away; behold, the new has come." Salvation is 100 percent God's work and 0 percent man's work. It cannot be anything else. If a person who is constantly trying to save him or herself because it seems like the right thing to do, and therefore says the words to be saved, most likely the work is man's work, not God's, and therefore impossible for true salvation. It is only when a person is drawn (urged) by the Holy Spirit can a person can be saved. That urge can be rejected by free will, which is the only work that free will can have in the salvation process. Grace saves while free will rejects salvation.

At the point of salvation, the Holy Spirit has entered into communication with our spirit (the baptism of the Spirit) and will never leave. He is the down payment and seal of our salvation and eternal life with God which will be completed when we enter into glory. Second Corinthians 1:21–22 tells us, "And it is God who establishes us with you in Christ, and has anointed us, and who has also put his seal on us and given us his Spirit in our hearts as a guarantee." This is all nonnegotiable, either with Satan and his demons or with mankind. It is eternal fact. The baptism of the Spirit is a spiritual work accomplished by the grace of God. It is not a physical happening and does not manifest itself in a physical way except for joy.

Now, after we are saved, we are suddenly given the responsibility to live for Christ. Ephesians 4:24 states, "Put on the new self, created after the likeness of God in true righteousness and holiness." A popular idea, both with newly saved and with unsaved, is that salvation is an end; that, when a person gets saved, he or she has arrived to the spiritual state of being a child of God, and will, at death or rapture, go to heaven, and there is no more that is necessary after salvation. The fact is that salvation is not an end of anything except the end of a life without Christ. Salvation is actually a beginning of a new life. That new life is a life of learning the Bible and acting out what is learned. It is so important that it takes a lifetime of continuous learning and lifestyle change and will never be complete until eternity. It is the focus of this study.

There is a very important point that needs to be considered regarding salvation. In the past one hundred years or so, it has become almost universal in Christian circles, to say that, after salvation, we have two natures, good and bad. What the Bible really teaches is that we have *a new nature*; the old nature is gone, never to return (Second Corinthians 5:17). The new nature, which is created in perfection by God, like Adam and Eve before sin entered the picture, is still capable of sinning, of self-centeredness, of acting in such a way that Satan is our lord rather than Jesus Christ. This happens because of compromise with the world or with worldly thinking. We are, in our new nature, capable of doing good or bad, depending upon how we "feed" that new nature. Just like Adam and Eve were created perfectly, with perfect freewill, but failed at their first temptation, failure is possible, often even 100 percent likely with us in our new nature. The memory of the previous life will come to play tricks on us and try to lead us back to a life of corruption. Satan will give us lies that are 90 percent truth and 10% lie to trick and mislead us. It is very important to fill that new nature with God via the Bible, meditation on what we have read in the Bible, and prayer (talking with God on a personal, intimate level, which He loves)! We must build that new house, our new nature, upon the foundation of rock, not of sand. Matthew 7:26–27 states, "And everyone who hears these words of mine and does not do them will be like a foolish man who built his house on the sand. And the rain fell, and the floods came, and the winds blew and beat against that house, and it fell, and great was the fall of it." This means that the foundation of our existence, our life, our reason for living, must be found in the teaching of God's eternal Word, not of our own ideas, thoughts and carnal acquaintances and traditions. We must consider the following passage.

> "When the unclean spirit has gone out of a person, it passes through waterless places seeking rest, but finds none. Then it says, 'I will return to my house from which I came.' And when it comes, it finds the house empty, swept, and put in order. Then it goes and brings with it seven other spirits more evil than itself, and they enter and dwell there, and the last state of that person is worse than the first. So also will it be with this evil generation" (Matthew 12:43–45).

The person ignored the urges of the Holy Spirit to fill himself with the Bible, prayer, fellowship with mature Christians, etc., and was therefore easy for the demon to conquer and destroy.

This is not to say that all unbelievers are demon possessed or that believers can become demon possessed (but unbelievers are children of Satan, and we all can be influenced by demons). The point is that a Christian not dedicated to his or her Lord will not be able to bear the affliction from the memory of worldly living and the demonic temptations *because* of the lack of feeding on the Word, prayer and meditation. This Bible passage makes very clear how important it is to fill our new natures with God and His Word. It is true that all unbelievers have Satan as their lord. Whenever believers do not honor Jesus Christ as our Lord by our thoughts, speech, and action, we are honoring Satan as our lord (Romans 6:16 is quoted below). The Holy Spirit will not force us to live according to God's Word; He will give us the power (grace) to reject Satan's ways *if* we choose to be obedient to God and His Word. All of this is to say that living by grace is living to honor God. Living by and for our self-centered desires, which corrupts our new nature, is living to honor Satan.

There are only two masters, or lords, in this world, in this universe, God Almighty, through Jesus Christ, and Satan. Every action or thought is towards one or the other master. No Christian is independent from either God or the Satanic realm. There is no time or instance when our thoughts or actions do not give honor to either one or the other, but never to both at the same time. The Bible tells us that whoever we choose to serve is our master. Romans 6:16 states, "Do you not know that if you present yourselves to anyone as obedient slaves [if you are obedient to a force or person], you are slaves of the one whom you obey, either of sin, which leads to death, or of obedience, which leads to righteousness?"

Please note that this exhortation, Romans 6:16, was not written to unbelievers but to believers! Does that mean that it is possible for a Christian to have any lord or master other than Jesus Christ? Absolutely! Self, when not controlled by the Holy Spirit, is a very powerful lord. When self is in control, Jesus Christ is not honored. That only leaves one other possibility, because, ultimately, there are only two lords in this universe. The first is Jesus Christ. The other is Satan:

> In their case the god of this world has blinded the minds of the unbelievers, to keep them from seeing the light of the gospel of the glory of Christ, who is the image of God... And no wonder, for even Satan disguises himself as an angel of light (Second Corinthians 4:4, 11:14).

Jesus Christ can only be our Lord if we make a decision of our will (by grace) to make Him our Lord by purposely living a life that honors God and is controlled by Him. Unfortunately, when we don't live a life pleasing to God, we do have Satan as our lord, even if we are saved. For an unbeliever, there is only one possible lord, which is Satan.

Matthew 6:24 states, "'No one can serve two masters, for either he will hate the one (Satan) and love the other (Jehovah God via Jesus Christ), or he will be devoted to the one (Satan) and despise the other (Jehovah God via Jesus Christ). You cannot serve God and money'" (riches, or whatever is more important than obeying God).

We would be remiss if we neglect to mention the first two commandments at this point,

> I am the LORD your God, who brought you out of the land of Egypt, out of the house of slavery. You shall have no other gods before me. You shall not make for yourself a carved image, or any likeness of anything that is in heaven above, or that is in the earth beneath, or that is in the water under the earth. You shall not bow down to them or serve them, *for I the LORD your God am a jealous God*, visiting the iniquity of the fathers on the children to the third and the fourth generation of those who hate me, but showing steadfast love to thousands of those who love me and keep my commandments (Exodus 20:2–6; emphasis added).

The personal question has to arise, who is *my* lord most of the time? If not Jesus Christ, why not?

Second Corinthians 10:5 states, "We destroy arguments and every lofty opinion raised against the knowledge of God, and take every thought captive to obey Christ,"

First Corinthians 10:12–13 tells us, "Therefore let anyone who thinks that he stands take heed lest he fall. No temptation has overtaken you that is not common to man. God is faithful, and he will not let you be tempted beyond your ability, but with the temptation he will also provide the way of escape, that you may be able to endure it."

The actual subject of this study is the four different potential stages in the life of a "born-again" believer in Christ. I call these steps

1. Surrender

2. Submission

3. Devotion and dedication (choosing to please God because we love Him)

4. Servant

The first two stages are necessary to being a Christian. It is impossible to be a Christian if these two stages are not achieved, one after the other. The last two potential stages seem to be reached only by the Christians who study the Bible diligently, to the point that these Christians, after a time of learning in Sunday school and church sermons, and hopefully from discipleship, begin to learn the Bible mostly by their own personal study, alone in a quiet place, and / or together with other Christians in a Bible study group which consists more of Bible study and discussion, than of fellowship, as important as fellowship is.

SURRENDER

To surrender is always a result of something happening. Many pastors or Bible teachers use the word *surrender* with an adjective, like *full* as in *full surrender*, to describe reaching the mature level of Christianity. There is nothing wrong with that. I am using the word in closer definition very simply because I want to go into greater detail discussing what others may refer to when saying *full surrender*.

When two factions, or parties, are at war (declared or otherwise), one faction decides that it cannot continue in the war any longer because of attrition, famine, severe losses, because fault was acknowledged, or being willing to give in because of being sick of war, etc. That faction or party surrenders. To surrender is very passive, even if it is an active act. It results in the inability, loss, or desire to continue, or acknowledging that the other faction was more powerful or correct. It is the result of the activity of the winning party, which is active. That is exactly what Ephesians 2:8–9 is about. The person who surrenders to God finds, by grace, that he or she cannot continue in a life without God, or, to look at the conversion of C. S. Lewis, the author of *The Chronicles of Narnia*, he could not keep fighting against God (*Surprised by Joy: The Shape of My Early Life*, by C. S. Lewis, London: Harvest Books, ISBN 978-0-15-687011-5, 1955, pg. 229).

The surrender of salvation must be a result of God's grace. It cannot be a self-centered desire of the person by his or her own freewill, or something one is talked into doing because it is the right thing to do as that kind freewill or coercion decision can easily be a *head knowledge* decision rather than a *heart* decision brought about by grace. If it is a *head knowledge* decision, it is not real salvation and, indeed, cannot be, as it is founded upon the person's efforts instead of upon God's work. God gives some excellent examples of *head knowledge* in the parable of the Sower in Matthew 13:3-9. In that parable, the Word of God is sown by the Holy Spirit in four different soils, the soils each representing a different way that people could react to God's saving grace.

"A sower went out to sow. And as he sowed, some seeds fell along the path, and the birds came and devoured them" (Matthew 13:3b-4). This is the first reaction to God's gospel. There is no salvation.

"Other seeds fell on rocky ground, where they did not have much soil, and immediately they sprang up, since they had no depth of soil, but when the sun rose they were scorched. And since they had no root, they withered away" (Matthew 13:5-6). In this second soil, the shallow soil over bedrock cannot hold the moisture needed to sustain the life of the seed [the Word of God]. The perceived salvation fails when "tribulation or persecution arises on account of the word" (verse 21), and no fruit is born.

"Other seeds fell among thorns, and the thorns grew up and choked them" (Matthew 13:7). In this third soil with seeds of thorns already in the ground, the perceived salvation always fails because the thorns grow and choke out life. The Word of God was accepted by a *"head knowledge"* decision and "the cares of the world and the deceitfulness of riches choke the word" (verse 24) and again, no fruit was born.

"Other seeds fell on good soil and produced grain, some a hundredfold, some sixty, some thirty" (Matthew 13:8). Only in the fourth soil, which had been prepared by grace, is there salvation; fruit is born.

Ephesians 2:8-9 tells us that true salvation is a passive experience which is caused by grace through faith, and neither grace nor faith is produced by ourselves. When grace is not rejected by a person's freewill, it penetrates and nullifies the individual's freewill so that grace can do its work. Then, at the right moment, God gives faith, which is the ability to react to the *heart knowledge* realization that the person is totally unacceptable to God, the person then realizing the need for a Savior by the faith given at that moment by our Lord, the sacrificial death of Jesus Christ, followed by His resurrection, is accepted, by God's grace. That decision of faith makes us acceptable to God by salvation through sacrificial death of Jesus Christ, who took the curse of sin, which is death, upon Himself, called the substitutional atonement, also called imputed righteousness. Imputed righteousness means that the perfect righteousness of Jesus Christ is given to us, put (imputed) into our account with God. After that action of salvation by grace happens, when God looks at one that He saved, even though that person is still an imperfect individual, He sees, in our place, the perfect righteousness of Jesus Christ, which is acceptable to God. By the God-given power of grace, through faith, the person is able to surrender to God and accept His plan of salvation. This experience is the baptism of the Spirit. It is the baptism of Ephesians 4:5. The baptism of the Spirit is the entry into the *one Body*, the body of Christ, "one body and one Spirit—just as you were called to the one hope that belongs to your call—one Lord, one faith, one baptism, one God and Father of all, who is over all and through all and in all" (Ephesians 4:4–6). Please note that the phrase "one baptism" does not mean *water* baptism or *believer* baptism. There can only be the baptism of the Holy Spirit, because, in the Greek, the particular word translated *one* in this instance means *one and only one* baptism. Believer baptism would have to be the second baptism.

The new believer experiences and learns the meaning of John 3:16: "For God so loved the world, that he gave his only Son, that whoever believes in him should not perish but have eternal life." The Christian gains great joy for a while as he or she experiences the love of God, never before experienced by that person, because the person has become a new creature, Second Corinthians 5:17. God introduces the new Christian into the fellowship of a local church and the fellowship love shown to him or her by that local church assembly. This new life in Christ is very immature and needs discipleship from one or more mature believers, which may or may not happen. This discipleship must teach the new believer that salvation is not an end; but is only the beginning of a new life with Christ and with fellow believers, a life of reading and learning the Bible, a life of worship and honoring God with his or her life, and a life of obedience and work to the glory of God. God exposes a few thoughts and activities that the new Christian has been involved in that are not suitable for a Christian, and helps the Christian to deal with those thoughts and activities. God may let the new Christian suffer some trials, tribulations, or persecution, which build Christian character.

I have seen new Christians get excited about their new life and want to get right out into the trenches to witness to old friends and lead others to the Lord. These new Christians have no foundation with which to fight against Satan and his demons, even though God limit's those evil powers. It is one thing to give a testimony of salvation. It is a different scenario to try to teach the Bible or teach others how to live a new life as a Christian. These new Christians need discipleship and large doses of Scripture to fill their mind with things of the Lord. If they go to the trenches, it should never be alone, but with experienced Christians. Satan and his demons are very alive and well in the presence of Christians, even though limited by God. "Now these things happened to them as an example, but they were written down for our instruction, on whom the end of the ages has come. Therefore let anyone who thinks that he stands take heed lest he fall" (First Corinthians 10:11–12).

Necessities for training new Christians:

- Have godly leadership and testimony: Titus 1:7–9 states, "For an overseer, as God's steward, must be above reproach. He must not be arrogant or quick-tempered or a drunkard or violent or greedy for gain, but hospitable, a lover of good, self-controlled, upright, holy, and disciplined. He must hold firm to the trustworthy word as taught, so that he may be able to give instruction in sound doctrine and also to rebuke those who contradict it."

- Teach the doctrines of Who God Is and how He helps the new Christian to understand and live the expected purity of the Body of Christ and fellowship with God and men: First John 1:5–10 states, "This is the message we have heard from him and proclaim to you, that God is light, and in him is no darkness at all. If we say we have fellowship with him while we walk in darkness, we lie and do not practice the truth. But if we walk in the light, as he is in the light, we have fellowship with one another, and the blood of Jesus his Son cleanses us from all sin. If we say we have no sin, we deceive ourselves, and the truth is not in us. If we confess our sins, he is faithful and just to forgive us our sins and to cleanse us from all unrighteousness. If we say we have not sinned, we make him a liar, and his word is not in us."

- Establish new believers in a Bible memory program to hide God's Word in their hearts.

- Establish the holiness of God, including the old hymns, also teaching the Satanic nature of most of CCM

(Contemporary Christian Music) which glorifies the "rock beat," and very often compromises true worship of God in the lyrics.

- Introduce the concept of the motivational spiritual gifts listed in Romans 12.

Necessities for the new Christian:

- Acts 17:11 states, "Now these Jews were more noble than those in Thessalonica; they received the word with all eagerness, examining the Scriptures daily to see if these things were so." The questions that arise from Bible study lead to understanding that is far beyond just reading the Bible, as long as the attitude is one of seeking God's wisdom and asking mature Christians who are well entrenched in the Word of God.

- Second Timothy 2:15 states, "Do your best (study) to present yourself to God as one approved, a worker who has no need to be ashamed, rightly handling the word of truth."

- First Thessalonians 5:17 states, "Pray without ceasing."

- Learn to hide the Word of God in their hearts.

- Learn to discern compromise in worship and living, and weed the improper from their lives and families.

SUBMISSION

Salvation must lead to submission, because salvation is not the act of the person. It is the act of God, by way of the love of God, the grace of God, the activity of the Holy Spirit, and the Word of God, all actively important to the life of the Christian.

Submission is where the saved person becomes active and starts to become useful to our Lord. Submission comes by learning that salvation is not an end, but a beginning, hearing the Word of God and learning that He did not save us so that we could go on in life as we had before Salvation. Ephesians 2:10 states, "For we are his workmanship, created in Christ Jesus for good works, which God prepared beforehand, that we should walk in them." The submission can be a very sudden realization that Jesus Christ suffered and died for our sins, and because of that, has become our Lord as well as our Savior, in which case that person will quickly move to stage 3. More often this submission is a slow spiritual growth of baby steps. In this stage of Christian living, we make decisions pleasing to God, such as, "I will regularly become a part of a local Bible teaching local church," and "I will regularly read the Bible." This Christian learns, through personal reading of God's Word, supported and interpreted by good preaching and teaching supported and encouraged by the Holy Spirit, that God has a very basic plan for all Christians. They plan is that God desires His people to be obedient to Him and worship Him. They must find that, to be obedient to Him starts with our giving up activities, friends and/or things that we like and enjoy, that interfere with our fellowship with God so that we can be obedient to God.

This phase of Christianity is basically learning the fundamentals of the Christian life while we learn to submit to God. The focus is on reading the Bible regularly, and as we grow, reading through the Bible on a regular basis, either from beginning to end or using a schedule. For myself, I started with small monthly devotional booklets, along with the recommended passages of the Bible. Then I started reading the Bible through, reading one book of history, then one book of prophesy, then one book of the New Testament, also reading through the books of poetry, checking off a list until I had read the Bible all the way through. I did this several times. Then I started reading the Bible all the way through from Beginning to End. Later I obtained a chronological Bible and read that all the way through several times, then back to reading the Bible beginning to end. Some people read through the Bible. They may find that God plants seeds into their minds. God uses these seeds as *rhemas* to develop plans in their lives. Others would rather study through the Bible to know God and His *logos*, to know God and to know and understand what is right and good and what is not. This, after years of study, teaches the student to see the world around him or her with a Biblical World View, which is God's wisdom.

The focus in the "submission" stage is also on becoming an active member of a local, Bible teaching church and what that entails. After worship, the focus is on becoming obedient as we learn the Word, which is a part of what worship is. Learning the Word is a goal in itself, which is also worship. Hosea states, in 6:6, "For I desire steadfast love and not sacrifice, the knowledge of God rather than burnt offerings." The Hebrew word translated "knowledge" means a full understanding and discernment based upon a solid relationship with God and His Word. Second Peter 1:1–4 tell us how to do it, and will be explained later in this chapter. During this stage, the Christian should learn the different *spiritual gifts* of Romans 12, not as *what* we do, but as the *motivator*, from God, to do what we do. There should also be some instruction in evangelism, but it should not be forced or coerced; this activity must be done through *love of God* and *love for the* lost, which is gained from personal time with God and His Word more than taught. Bible based discipleship is very important in this stage with a mature Christian or in a small group, focused first upon accurate understanding of the Bible, and on Christian fellowship. The discipleship should also include exposing the new Christian to different ministries in the local church. Ignorance is generally not the fault of the new Christian (unless he or she refuses to participate and learn); it is the fault of the ministry and administration of the local church fellowship.

I still remember when I left the denomination of my heritage and joined a Biblically and socially conservative church. In a short period of time the elderly, retired pastor in charge of calling upon people for different reasons put his arm of love around this immature but growing Christian and included me in his work, as he saw that I had a heart for the Lord. That little effort on his part accomplished several things. It made me feel welcomed and pulled me into true fellowship in that local church body. It helped me to get to know some of the mature members of that body of Christ. It also exposed me to a ministry that was very centered upon the Bible, which still influences me today. This kind of sharing love is rare today.

Congregational leaders should pay more attention to First Corinthians 12:18: "But as it is, God arranged the members in the body, each one of them, as he chose." God plants certain chosen people into every congregation, often because of the lack of specific *spiritual gifts*, and sometimes for the new person to be trained and discipled. This activity of God is too often a very, very threatening and uncomfortable occurrence for the current administration, especially since these spiritual gifts in Romans 12 are motivators from God, not just things that the administration wants the person to do. The question has to be asked, "Whose church is this?" Too often the wrong answer is presented, following the pattern of the Pharisees of Jesus's day.

It is a sin before our All-Knowing, All-Powerful God Almighty, when a new Christian comes to the congregation and is not discipled and used for God's glory. Yes, the administration has the duty and authority to make sure that the person's theology is correct. But, too often, this type of new member was sent by God and is ignored by the current administration, which thinks it has everything under control, and thus misses out on the great love and desires that our holy and righteous God has for that local congregation. It is no wonder that the power that God intends for the local church is seldom manifested in the way God desires. Luke 20:18 can be applied to many local congregations, "Everyone who falls on that stone will be broken to pieces, and when it falls on anyone, it will crush him." To put it another way, things done by God's leading will often cause painful change, but things accomplished by free will of the administrators will restrain God's work; it will be crushed. If we do things by God's way (Biblical principles, commands, and the leading of the Holy Spirit), we may face problems and trials (be broken to pieces), but God will always re-assemble the congregation to be stronger in the Lord and therefore more useful to His desires.

As we grow in being obedient through submission, we learn the concept of becoming submissive to Jesus Christ our Lord. We may find that we cannot remain silent about our salvation, and we give testimony to and share the Gospel with old friends, relatives, and others. In this, we have to learn how to use grace and faith that God has blessed us with. Acting without learning how to use grace is often futile and must be learned, along with all of the new life in Christ. This is one of the reasons why discipleship and learning the spiritual gifts are so important.

In this stage, we begin to learn the two kinds of love that God desires in Christian fellowship, *agape* and *phileo*. Before we learn these concepts, our understanding of the word *love* is, to English speaking people at least, extremely misleading and often corrupted. In the English, we have one word that, in the Greek is understood and used by four different words. The New Testament uses two of these words in the family of God and its activities, neither of which is the romantic love that should be between spouses. The first Greek word for love is transliterated *agape* (noun; *agapeo* is the verb). This form of love is, for the most part, missing in the English. The second Greek word for love in Christian fellowship used in the Bible is *phileo*. *Phileo* is not really thought of as love in our English language tradition, although in the local assembly and the Universal Body of Christ, it should be.

Agape love is the love that God showed in the sacrificial atonement of Jesus Christ for our benefit: Romans 5:8 states, "but God shows his love for us in that while we were still sinners, Christ died for us." This love, used in the Biblical manner, is nonexistent outside of Christianity. The characteristics are

- It is an act of the will, not of emotions. It will not be *agape* if is an act of our self-centered *free will* which is always adverse to God's will that He plants in us.

- It will always involve personal sacrifice, in time spent, in value of monetary nature, in use of possessions or purchased items to be given, or any combination, in the exercise of this love.

- It will always be for the benefit of the anticipated target of this love, as seen through the eyes of God. This benefit is not necessarily what the recipient wants, but will be what the recipient needs in the biblical worldview. In other words

  o Will God be glorified?

○   Will the target be led closer to God through the reception and acceptance of this love (this is why it is nonexistent outside of Christianity)?

○   Will the target be lifted up spiritually or harmed spiritually in the exercise of this love?

○   When given to someone who would waste it or use it unwisely this action cannot be *agapeo* love, even though it may involve personal sacrifice and is intended by the giver for good.

• It will always have the goal of leading someone to Christ or closer to God through Jesus Christ.

• It will often involve just being with someone who needs the closeness of true friendship, and sometimes involves giving Biblical guidance and/or discipleship.

• It will often involve the use of a "spiritual gift" which God has energized individually to the Christian exercising that love. God places every true Christian in any particular situation for a purpose which may involve what God gifted us with (First Corinthians 12:18). Sensing the burden that the Holy Spirit loads us with counts greatly in this, which is why it is so important to be pure, having a very short list of unforgiven sins (the list cannot be any shorter than empty) of which we need to repent and ask God and often other people, to forgive us.

• The King James Version often calls *agape* love "charity," which is quite accurate.

Phileo (pronounced fil-lay'-oh) is another kind of love mentioned in the Bible for love in Christian fellowship. Technically, *fileo* is the non romantic, nonsexual personality attraction for another person because they have something in common, such as liking horses, motorcycles, books, etc. In the Bible, it is used for Christian fellowship, the personal attraction of one Christian to another because of our mutual love of God and the fellowship of believers. We Christians have the bond of Christ, being part of the family of God, which should bind us together. Stronger yet is the bond of Christians working together in any particular local church body or group. That bond is *phileo*. When persecution of Christians arises, that bond gets very, very close, in a non romantic, nonsexual way. Of course, purity is to be part of the character of a Christian, and care must be taken so the *phileo* love does not get carried into unhealthy involvement.

A related concept of these forms of Christian love is "fellowship", transliterated *koinonia,* which English word "fellowship" is used in the New Testament twelve times. It is the working out of Christian love in a group setting, closely related to *phileo*. Regarding fellowship, we are instructed to:

- Have fellowship with God and His Word (First Corinthians 9; Ephesians 3:9; Philippians. 2:1, 3:1; 1 John 1:3).

- Have fellowship with each other (Acts 2:42, Second Corinthians 8:4, 2 Cor. 8:4, Galatians 2:9, Philippians 1:5, 1 John 1:7).

- Do not have fellowship (First Corinthians 10:20, Second Corinthians 6:14, Ephesians 5:11).

- Please review these verses in your own Bible; they are excellent in meaning.

In this submission stage of spiritual growth, we begin to understand, in our hearts, God's love for us. Much of what we have learned, from the Bible and from Bible teachers is head knowledge that must be transferred to the heart. All spiritual growth comes from the Word, taught to us by the Holy Spirit through our own study and learning from Bible teachers that God puts into our path of life. We begin to meditate on the Word of God that we are learning. The Greek word translated as *meditate* pictures some mammals *chewing the cud.* It is bringing up to our mind things that we have learned and making it real to us, which is how we learn to understand it and make it a part of our lives. Problems that God allows to occur in our lives, along with meditation of His Word, makes God's Word a real part of us that we need to learn to effectively lean on God and His Word in this life. We know about God's grace in an elementary sense but really don't have a good understanding of it and how necessary it is to a Christian's life in order to live a life pleasing to Him. We may think we know the spiritual gifts but really have not much experienced the great joy that we receive in the outworking of those gifts. Our fellowship with God is immature; we don't have a vibrant life with Him. In John 10:10b Jesus tells us, "I came that they[you] may have life and have it abundantly." We must learn to *listen* and *obey* God's Word before that vibrant life of great personal fellowship with God can be realized.

> If you keep my commandments, you will abide in my love, just as I have kept my Father's commandments and abide in his love. These things I have spoken to you, that my joy may be in you, and that your joy may be full. "This is my commandment, that you love one another as I have loved you. Greater love has no one than this, that someone lays down his life for his friends. You are my friends if you do what I command you. No longer do I call you servants, for the servant does not know what his master is doing; but I have called you friends, for all that I have heard from my Father I have made known to you (John 15:10–15).

We begin to experience some joy. Happiness is not joy, happiness is an emotion because something happened. Joy is the result of a way of life that comes by choosing to live a life of obedience to God's commands and principles as given in His Word.

It seems that the majority of people who call themselves Christians live in the surrender and submission stage. Many don't seem to *graduate* from submission because they are acting by way of their own freewill, feeling a *duty* to submit to love of God and His Word, instead of permitting God's grace to work in and through them so that they can realize that "my yoke is easy, and my burden is light" (Matthew 11:30) and have that desire to possess the love of God and His Word. These people who call themselves Christians (and may be saved) have not learned that much time must be spent in *quiet time*, set aside on purpose to spend that time with God in

His Word, meditation and prayer. To them, that time of *devotions* is not a labor of love or something we have joy in but is something that we feel that we have to do. For the true Christian, this "quiet time" needs to include, not just reading through the Bible in whatever organization one chooses but also needs to include studying, praying and meditating on the Bible to know, understand and apply it to our lives. Maybe most Christians don't choose to spend the time to do this. Or maybe these people are not saved, as they are rejecting the work, the grace of the Holy Spirit, part of whose job is to encourage us to spend time in the Word. The false believers think that they are saved, possibly because of the sloppy work of an evangelist. They see salvation as an end rather than as a beginning.

As true Christians get near the end of this phase, they will begin learning the Biblical worldview. Very simply, this is seeing activities in politics, the world in general, friends, personal and group activities, work, etc., as God sees them. This can be quite an eye opener, and it can be somewhat painful. They begin to see that they must quit having fellowship with some of the friends and activities from before their salvation. At the same time, they begin to see Christianity in a new light and develop new relationships. It is an exciting time of change.

My belief, based upon Romans 6–8, is that every true Christian will accept Jesus Christ as Lord as well as Savior before he or she dies (Romans 8:29–35; John 15), unless God wills that we die a physical death before that can happen.

> For those whom he foreknew he also predestined to be conformed to the image of his Son, in order that he might be the firstborn among many brothers. And those whom he predestined he also called, and those whom he called he also justified, and those whom he justified he also glorified. What then shall we say to these things? If God is for us, who can be against us? He who did not spare his own Son but gave him up for us all, how will he not also with him graciously give us all things? Who shall bring any charge against God's elect? It is God who justifies. Who is to condemn? Christ Jesus is the one who died—more than that, who was raised—who

is at the right hand of God, who indeed is interceding for us. Who shall separate us from the love of Christ? Shall tribulation, or distress, or persecution, or famine, or nakedness, or danger, or sword (Romans 8:29–35)?

If we, after salvation, harden our hearts to the Lord without repentance, He will, on His timetable take us out of the world early so that we do not "drag His name in the mud" during this lifetime.

- "Do not quench the Spirit" (First Thessalonians 5:19).

- "That is why many of you are weak and ill, and some have died" (First Corinthians 11:30).

A warning is in order at this time. Saying the words of salvation and praying the prayer do not make one saved. True salvation comes only when the heart has been moved and prepared by God to let God be in control by letting the Holy Spirit guide and teach. The proof of salvation is the working of the Holy Spirit in and through each Christian.

For if you live according to the flesh [your own free will] you will die, but if by the Spirit you put to death the deeds of the body, you will live. For all who are led by the Spirit of God are sons of God. For you did not receive the spirit of slavery to fall back into fear, but you have received the Spirit of adoption as sons, by whom we cry, "Abba! Father!" The Spirit himself bears witness with our spirit that we are children of God, and if children, then heirs—heirs of God and fellow heirs with Christ, provided we suffer with him in order that we may also be glorified with him (Romans 8:13–17).

If the Christian does not experience the work of the Holy Spirit in his/her life, then that person is not a true Christian. If the works of the Holy Spirit is not known in a person's life, he or she cannot be a Christian.

- "The Spirit himself bears witness with our spirit that we are children of God" Romans 8:16.

- "If anyone does not abide in me he is thrown away like a branch and withers; and the branches are gathered, thrown into the fire, and burned (John 15:6).

- "They went out from us, but they were not of us; for if they had been of us, they would have continued with us. But they went out, that it might become plain that they all are not of us (First John 2:19).

Again, see a parable from Matthew 13:24–30, the wheat and tares.

> He put another parable before them, saying, "The kingdom of heaven may be compared to a man who sowed good seed in his field, but while his men were sleeping, his enemy came and sowed weeds among the wheat and went away. So when the plants came up and bore grain, then the weeds appeared also. And the servants of the master of the house came and said to him, 'Master, did you not sow good seed in your field? How then does it have weeds?' He said to them, 'An enemy has done this.' So the servants said to him, 'Then do you want us to go and gather them?' But he said, 'No, lest in gathering the weeds you root up the wheat along with them. Let both grow together until the harvest, and at harvest time I will tell the reapers, Gather the weeds first and bind them in bundles to be burned, but gather the wheat into my barn.'"

Some false Christians realize that they are plants of Satan to cause confusion and dissension in the local body of Christ, but most think that they are saved. They can be Sunday school teachers, members of the board, and even pastors. Jesus warns us, in Matthew 7:21–23 that not everyone who thinks that they are saved are actually saved:

> "Not everyone who says to me, 'Lord, Lord,' will enter the kingdom of heaven, but the one who does the will of my Father who is in heaven. On that day many will

say to me, 'Lord, Lord, did we not prophesy in your name, and cast out demons in your name, and do many mighty works in your name?' And then will I declare to them, 'I never knew you; depart from me, you workers of lawlessness.'"

How can this happen that a person who seems to have gone through the salvation process is not saved? It can easily happen because they were "saved" by their own work instead of God's.

While I was in a retail store, I met a man who I found was a pastor of a local congregation which is all about emotions, works, and "signs and wonders" but did not know the Bible. He knew the different *baptisms* of his belief system (all but one of the them being based upon things that demon worshipers may do, such as voicing unintelligent, meaningless sounds, being able to *interpret* these unholy sounds, being *slain by the spirit*, etc.) but did not know the Bible well enough to be considered a mature Christian. He kept on coming up with his unbiblical *baptisms of the spirit*, which I told him were not Biblical, but may well be demonic. I also told him, several times, to "read the Bible!" He gave me what he considered the proof of the work of the Holy Spirit in his life. He said he needed something which was to be found in only one retail store in another city. He knew the city that the store was in but did not know where the store was in that city. He said he asked God to show him where the store was, and started to drive and went right to the store! He said that was God's work! It may have been God or a demon or could easily have been coincidence that brought him to the store. But it surely was not a good proof that he was a Christian, much less a mature Christian. If that very weak incident was his proof of salvation, I pity him. He could not tell me what good he was to the edification of the body of Christ, to his family, or to his faith because of the work of the Holy Spirit in his life. He could not. I am not God; I cannot say, for sure, that the pastor was not saved, but I can certainly say that I would fear for his salvation, in spite of his being a pastor.

Saying the words and praying the prayer of salvation do not make a person saved; the presence of the Holy Spirit in that person's life, actively working in and through him or her, does show that a person is saved; this is what the book of James is about. When there is the presence of the Holy Spirit, there will also be the work of the Holy Spirit, unless the person is quenching the Holy Spirit (First Thessalonians 5:19). True salvation *only* happens when the salvation is God's work, not when that person's work is his or her own work. Only true believers go on to the next stage.

The necessities for both the local church and the growing Christians, regarding the ongoing spiritual maturity of these Christians are the same as before, but adding what it means to be humble and meek.

Also, it is very, very important that the Christians be given some responsible duties in the function of the local church, both general duties and duties that fit their motivational gifts. These duties should never be greater than the ability to function for these growing Christians; the idea to keep in mind is that they are immature Christians who need ongoing guidance and training to become mature Christians.

DEVOTION AND DEDICATION:

As we spend time in the Word, by our own study and by listening to Bible teachers, we begin to understand God's love for us. By this time, we should be learning and understanding God's Word and applying it to our life walk than we learn from the teaching and preaching in the local fellowship. We experience and realize what God can do in and through us because we have been saved (the proof of salvation is the work of the Holy Spirit in and through us to grow us spiritually and to draw others to Christ or closer to Christ). We have learned that we cannot, with our own corruptible will and our own efforts, to even begin to please God. We learn and are still learning, to take God's will upon us by grace, and by grace, choose to put aside our corrupted, self-centered will. Before we reached this stage we learned that God loves us. Now, we are learning to love God more than we love ourselves. We learn to become devoted, dedicated to Christ our Lord and to God the Father through our Lord. We begin to experience, in our heart and lives, the truth that God loves us, and we, in turn, love God and want to live a life that is actually pleasing to God. This is where the Christian begins to live what we find in Ephesians chapters 4 through 6 and John chapters 10–17, among many other Bible passages. It is passing from childish immaturity to maturity in our spiritual lives.

Jesus gives us a very violent word picture to show the difference between what will happen to the unsaved, and what needs to happen to a person so that he or she can be saved.

Luke 12:49–51 states, "I came to cast fire on the earth, and would that it were already kindled! I have a baptism to be baptized with, and how great is my distress until it is accomplished! Do you think that I have come to give peace on earth? No, I tell you, but rather division."

Matthew 10:34, 38–40 states, "Do not think that I have come to bring peace to the earth. I have not come to bring peace, but a sword... And whoever does not take his cross and follow me is not worthy of me. Whoever finds his life will lose it, and whoever loses his life for my sake will find it. Whoever receives you receives me, and whoever receives me receives him who sent me."

Jesus told the Chief Priests and Pharisees, "And the one who falls on this stone will be broken to pieces; and when it falls on anyone, it will crush him" (Matthew 21:44, also Luke 20:18). We can paraphrase this to say, to be a believer in Jesus Christ, one must be broken from the self-centeredness of putting ourselves in place of God, thereby permitting God to re-form us into who He intended us to be. If this does not happen, we are not truly Christians. If we do not submit to that breaking, we will be removed from this earth early or we will be destroyed for eternity, separated from God, in hell. It takes the brokenness from self-centeredness to be saved. The alternative is ongoing, never ceasing, destruction for eternity in hell.

Jesus Christ gave us a perfect example of brokenness when He came to earth in His humanity. If we look at that famous passage in Philippians 2:5–8, we find that Jesus, in order to live as a true man emptied Himself of being God (called the *kenosis* – the self-emptying of Christ) without ceasing, in any way, to be God. This act of *kenosis* was absolutely necessary for him to become the once and for all sacrifice acceptable to the Father to save, or deliver, us from our sins (John 3:16; Hebrews 10:10; First Peter 3:18), become children of God (John 1:12) and have eternal life with our God. It was the suffering and death of His perfect humanity that saved us, not His being God.

Sidebar: Other scholars call this passage in Philippians the *hyperstatic union*, which is making something that had never existed before by God's joining humanity to Jesus, not changing His being God in any way, but adding humanity to his being God, part of the Trinity for eternity past, present and future. That humanity has never left Jesus. Both the *kenosis* and the *hyperstatic union* are correct; it need not be one or the other.

Sidebar 2: Jesus was not known in the Old Testament, although He was prophesied. He, the eternal second Person of the Trinity of God, was known only as the Angel of God or the Captain of the Host (armies) of God in the Old Testament. Acts 13:32-33 states, "And we bring you the good news that what God promised to the fathers, this he has fulfilled to us their children by raising Jesus, as also it is written in the second Psalm, 'You are my Son, today I have begotten you.'" The eternal second Person of the Trinity became the only begotten Son of God when He laid aside His Godhood, never ceasing to be God, became human, was born of the virgin Marry, was named Jesus and who was the prophesied Messiah (God with us). He gave us His Word of the New Testament, fulfilled many Old Testament prophesies, became, through suffering and death, the once and for all eternal sacrificial Passover Lamb, and now sits in Heaven, at the right hand of the Father, still as the human Son of God, but never ceasing to be God. He is our intercessor with the Father, who loves us so much that He wants that intercession for us. Second Corinthians 5:17-19 tells us that "if anyone is in Christ, he is a new creation. The old has passed away; behold, the new has come. All this is from God, who through Christ reconciled us to himself and gave us the ministry of reconciliation; that is, in Christ God was reconciling the world to himself, not counting their trespasses against them, and entrusting to us the message of reconciliation."

If we do the same *kenosis* with ourselves (possible only by grace), by emptying ourselves of being our self-centered selves, which the Bible calls being crucified with Christ (Galatians 2:20; Romans 6:3–7) or dying to self (First Corinthians 15:31, 36), and taking upon us the commands and principles of God, learned from His Word and taught to us by the Holy Spirit, all of which is the will of God, we, too, can please God. This is actual righteousness, which is impossible by our own efforts, but is what God expects of us. He never, never intended any saved person to remain the same as when that person received salvation. God is a good businessman; He expects a return from His investment. His investment was the passion and death of Jesus Christ for our benefit (Matthew 12:33, 13:8, 25:14–30; Luke 13:6–9; John 15:8). In a Christian's life, when we, by grace, permit the Holy Spirit to dwell in and with us to produce actual righteousness, we are entering into the stage of life that begins to please God. Another way to say it is that living by grace is what it takes to produce fruit, internal and external, which is God's will for all of mankind, but possible only in those who, by the grace and the faith which He gives, believe. In doing this self-emptying, we do not lose our character, our personality. Hopefully, by grace we purge the self-centeredness out of our personality (we die daily, First Corinthians 15:31). God created a specific personality for each one of us for a purpose and gave it to us at conception (my personal belief is that God gave us, at conception, what would become motivational *spiritual gifts*, which He *switches on* when we are saved. We just need to mature that personality in actual righteousness, possible only by grace.

When we permit God's grace to work in us, by "*kenosis*" (self-emptying of self by grace) and being controlled by the Spirit (Ephesians 5:9–21), we begin to live the joyful life of a child of God, in spite of what suffering, trial or tribulation we may be experiencing.

Because we are spending quality time in the Bible and prayer, and because we are submitted to our Lord and being devoted to Him, we begin to see miraculous things happen because of God in our lives.

Some examples of living by God's will are *coincidental* meetings with other people in which they are blessed by your being there and talking with them. Other examples are when you feel an urge to pray for someone or to meet with someone, and God works in miraculous ways because of your obedience. Or it could be that the Holy Spirit is leading for God's work to be accomplished for His glory, the edification of some of His saints, and even for salvation of unbelievers.

A few actual examples are:

- You move to a new area and find, over an hour's drive away, in a small conservative Bible Church, an group of Christian men, including the pastor, who are trying to start a Bible institute. You already knew the pastor and one of the men and join them, offering the necessary spiritual maturity and wisdom to get the Bible institute going. In the small first group of graduates, 60 percent go directly into church leadership as pastors, one of which quit his successful employment and goes to a famous Bible seminary, graduating to become a pastor. The balance of graduates (none did not graduate) had grown stronger in family leadership and in ministry in their local churches. Several thanked you for the needed boost to guide and encourage them and the one who went on to seminary sees you as his spiritual father, even though he was already saved when you joined.

- You were teaching an adult class in Sunday school. That day, you taught the Abrahamic covenant in its entirety. At the end of the class, a man your age, a Christian Jew who had lived to adulthood in Israel, came to you and thanked you for that lesson. He told you that, in Israel, what we know as the Abrahamic covenant was taught as history. He had never understood God's promise and work in the Abrahamic covenant that was so obvious the way you had taught it.

- You are a corporate engineer in a large business and travel a lot to do projects in manufacturing plants in several states. In a couple of the plants, you find Christians who are hungry for Christian fellowship. At one plant, there is a small core group of Christians that also includes one unbeliever who thinks he is a Christian. He is loved with God's love just as if he were a true Christian, but also given a few nonthreatening, leading passages from the Bible. Several months later you make a trip to that plant and walk the plant to see how things are going. You haven't seen the unbeliever for over a year. In a part of the plant which you have never worked before, you see that unbeliever, but there is a very noticeable change in his appearance and demeanor. He sees you and comes right over with a great big smile on his face and says, "[Your name], I got saved!" Then you two had fellowship as brothers in Christ, which was very, very wonderful. He had very quickly come to this third level of Christian spiritual growth. That is not to say that his life was easy; it wasn't. But he had eternal salvation and that great joy of full fellowship with his God and with God's people.

These are just a few examples of the many ways that a dedicated, devoted Christian can be used by God. This represents some of the ways that the Joy of the Lord *will* be experienced when fully devoted! This is the Holy Spirit bearing witness with our spirit. This is what Peter was talking about in Second Peter 1:3–4, where he uses the word *knowledge*. The Greek word Peter used is not the common word for knowledge, which is transliterated *ginosko*, Strong's #1097. Instead, God, through Peter, used the word that greatly intensified knowledge to full discernment & understanding, transliterated *epignosis*, Strong's #1922,

> His divine power has granted to us all things that pertain to life and godliness, through the knowledge of him who called us to his own glory and excellence, by which he has granted to us his precious and very great promises,

so that through them you may become partakers of the divine nature, having escaped from the corruption that is in the world because of sinful desire.

Please note that none of the above examples, along with many more, happened because you thought that you ought to do such and such. Each of these occurrences, among many others, was totally God's work and not your own; you just happened to be the prepared tool that God chose to use in God's timing. God was in total control of the circumstances, even to the words that came out of your mouth. That is grace. We can and will experience the grace, the love of God, and our love for Him, in our life when we are devoted, dedicated to Him. The most important ingredient to experience this grace is very explicitly given in John 14:21: "Whoever has my commandments and keeps them, he it is who loves me. And he who loves me will be loved by my Father, and I will love him and manifest myself to him."

John 15:7–14 tells us,

If you abide in me, and my words abide in you, ask whatever you wish, and it will be done for you. By this my Father is glorified, that you bear much fruit and so prove to be my disciples. As the Father has loved me, so have I loved you. Abide in my love. If you keep my commandments, you will abide in my love, just as I have kept my Father's commandments and abide in his love. These things I have spoken to you, that my joy may be in you, and that your joy may be full. "This is my commandment, that you love one another as I have loved you. Greater love has no one than this, that someone lays down his life for his friends. You are my friends *if you do what I command you.*"

When we submit to the Lordship of Jesus Christ, in obedience, because we love Him, because we are devoted and dedicated to Him, we find our fellowship with our Lord grow further than any logic can measure; we find that our friendship with other Christians grows more rich (*phileo* love of the brethren). We find that God, who gave *agape* love to us at Salvation, uses each of us to spread that *agape* love in the place in which He has planted us. We find that our lives become more fulfilled, meaningful, and joyful. Jesus, in John 10:10b, tells us, "I came that they may have life and have it abundantly."

Spiritual gifts were mentioned previously in this study. The spiritual gifts that God mentions in Romans 12 are different than other lists of gifts or spiritual fruit or development. The gifts in Romans 12 are not what we do but what urges or causes us to do what we do. These gifts are personal motivators, given by God, specifically to do God's will. They cannot be controlled by anyone except God the Holy Spirit (except to deny it's use). The different gifts are not isolated. They are a part of a whole. God puts so much emphasis in these gifts that he says, in First Corinthians 12:18, "But as it is, God arranged [set or placed] the members in the body, each one of them, as he chose."

Spiritual gifts should never be a mystery. Even before I knew about this third stage of spiritual growth, many people from different parts of my city, county, and state, and from different walks of life, told me what my main gift is. I rejected what they all said without further thought. "There is no way I can do that," I told myself. And do you know what? I was right. After I entered into this third phase of Christianity, long before I realized that it was the third phase, I began to realize the motivating spiritual gift that God gave me, even though I had never though I never wanted it. It was because God was pushing me in that direction, which, as I matured in understanding God's Word, became a very strong motivator and desire in my life, not because others had told me and continued to tell me but because God put that drive into me, that same drive very aptly mentioned in Jeremiah 20:9b and 23:29a and Ezekiel 22:30; that drive that drove me (a labor of love) into intense Bible study for years; that drive that, after much study, drove me and still drives me to teach what I had learned and still continue to learn.

- Jeremiah 20:9b states, "…There is in my heart as it were a burning fire shut up in my bones, and I am weary with holding it in, and I cannot."

- Jeremiah 23:29a states, "Is not my word like fire? declares the LORD..."

- God said, in Ezekiel 22:30, "And I sought for a man among them who should build up the wall and stand in the breach before me for the land, that I should not destroy it, but I found none."

I, through His leading by grace, in humility and meekness before God, told Him that I wanted to be, would be that man that God searched for. And He has used me as such over and over and over again, and is still using me as I write this study.

Numerous people have verified it. God, Himself, has verified it. The only mystery to spiritual gifts is the lack of obedience to God and His Word. When a person is maturing in this third potential stage of a Christian's life, the spiritual gift(s) become obvious to other mature Christians and to the particular Christian him or herself.

In this third potential stage of a Christian's life, the spiritual gifts mature. When God sees that a local congregation is lacking in an area, He moves a person with the necessary spiritual gift to that local congregation (remember First Corinthians 12:18).

- error, sin, evil is uncovered to be dealt with per Matthew 18:15–20 (gift of prophecy). Please note that God puts more emphasis on the purity of the local church congregation than He does on evangelism! Why? Because evangelism comes as a by-product of a healthy local church, but error, sin or evil thinking, thoughts or action kill the spiritual health of a local church.

- people are freed from work that is keeping them from God's work for the glory of God and the edification of the saints and salvation of souls (gift of service, helping). The helper gets great joy from being able to free people to do what God wants them to do.

- the members of the congregation grow strong in maturity and life in Christ (teacher). This teacher, which is the same as the teacher in Ephesians 4:11, is specifically a person who God has gifted with good Bible knowledge and understanding of Bible doctrine along with the God-given ability to teach it in a way that is easy for others to understand. The teacher is a person who God called and empowered to keep Bible doctrine highly honored in worship and practice and has the motivation to study, study, study and spend much time in meditation on what he or she has studied.

- doctrine or principles are broken down into easy to understand steps and put into practice, a little at a time, so that some or all can grow in the Lord (exhorter). The exhorter is enabled break Bible doctrine or principles into small baby steps that confused or troubled people are able to take to reach the new heights of Christian service.

- financial activities and goals are corrected and found attainable, along with increased giving to meet the goals (contributor or giver). The giver, for the most part, seems to have the ability to turn most all of their efforts into financial success due to God's grace and direction. It is from the giver that much of God's "cattle upon a thousand hills" comes from (Psalms. 50:10b).

- goals, projects, service, and worship are created and organized for efficiency and order (leader). The leader is given the gift of organization and therefore is often an administrator. The person with this gift is often elevated to a supervisory or leadership position because of the near perfect memory and ability to organize that come with this gift. This gift often misused by immature people with this gift, as the person so gifted gets to think that he or she is the only gifted person in the assembly, where God specifically wants this person to recognize and benefit all by understanding that the other spiritual gifts are equally important to his or her own.

- healing needs to occur after a person guilty of committing sin that hurts the congregation is recognized. Discipline initiated upon Matthew 18:15-20 must be used to bring about repentance. After repentance must come restoration. Some people don't think that there should be restoration which brings a lack of forgiveness. Healing occurs through the tremendous work of mercy of the healer, whom is often called Mercy. Mercy very naturally wants to heal the hurt before God is ready for the hurt to be healed. Mercy must wait until the work of the other six gifts is completed to make ready for restoration. Then comes the fantastic, fabulous, miraculous work of healing.

Please note that when the Christian is able to exercise his or her gifts, along with the mature devotion and dedication brought about by our love of our Savior for who He is and what He has done, there is spiritual health and agreement in the local assembly. Why? Because God is control, not we ourselves! The working of spiritual gifts is accomplished by the Holy Spirit. The use of spiritual gifts is Spirit energized, Spirit led and Spirit used for the edification of the local assembly and, sometimes for the benefit of the Universal Church. It is grace. The importance of spiritual gifts cannot be emphasized, as it is God's work, just like salvation is God's work. Leading people to the salvation of their souls is also a natural result of the working of spiritual gifts, because we are not just including God to enter into *our* work; we are, instead, entering into *God's* work, doing God's work God's way. This all comes naturally, as a by-product of a close walk with our Lord when we are free to exercise our spiritual gifts; it is grace; it is the working of God in our lives and congregations; it is God who is in control.

Warren Wiersbe is one of the modern heroes of Bible teaching. This quote is from his book, *The Bible Exposition Commentary* (volume 1, Victor Books, Wheaton, IL 60189, a division of Scripture Press Publications, Inc., 1989, pg. 554) regarding the spiritual gifts in Romans 12.

The basic idea is that each believer is a living part of Christ's body, and each one has a spiritual function to perform. Each believer has a gift (or gifts) to be used for the building up of the body and the perfecting of the other members of the body. In short, we belong to each other, we minister to each other, and we need each other. What are the essentials for spiritual ministry and growth in the body of Christ?

Honest evaluation (v 3). Each Christian must know what his spiritual gifts are and what ministry (or ministries) he is to have in the local church. It is not wrong for a Christian to recognize gifts in his own life and in the lives of others. What is wrong is the tendency to have a false evaluation of ourselves. Nothing causes more damage in a local church than a believer who overrates himself and tries to perform a ministry that he cannot do (sometimes the opposite is true, and people undervalue themselves. Both attitudes are wrong.)

The gifts that we have came because of God's grace. They must be accepted and exercised by faith. We are saved "by grace, through faith" (Ephesians 2:8–9), and we must live and serve "by grace through faith." Since our gifts are from God, we cannot take the credit for them. All we can do is accept them and use them to honor His name (See First Corinthians 15:10 for Paul's personal testimony about gifts).

Spiritual gifts are important enough to God that He supernaturally works through them, when He is permitted, by the local church, to do so. Many leaders severely limit what more can be done if spiritual are free to work. Leadership that is devoted and dedicated in *submission* to the Lordship of Jesus Christ, emptying self of self so that God can be permitted to be God, permit God to make great things happen for His glory, for the edification of saints, and for the salvation of souls, all by grace. When God is in control, and grace is allowed to work, God's work is done more fully. The members of the congregation grow to greater spiritual maturity, which is this potential stage of the Christian's growth, the side effect is that many people get saved. This is the Biblical way of fulfilling the great commission.

The salvation of the unsaved is a side effect, or automatic benefit of the very important factors of worship which includes growing in doctrinal understanding, grace and selflessness. The exercising of spiritual gifts probably has more to do with each individual Christian's exercise of leading souls to salvation than anything else that can come into play in a local church, because it is the exercising of these motivational gifts of Romans 12 that makes the Christian compete. The opposite is very true; not exercising God-given spiritual gifts of grace will deprive a Christian of much joy and usefulness. The spiritual gift very much defines the way the person thinks. If the spiritual gift(s) is not used, the thought process for that person is incomplete and his or her service to the Lord and His people is incomplete. Remember that spiritual gifts are part of God's grace, the working of His grace in a way that He, when freed by the local administration, orchestrates. Limiting the work of these spiritual gifts is absolutely limiting grace. Every local church that does not encourage the exercise of spiritual gift is depriving that local body of *much* of God's favor, energy and desired results. If we stop to think about this, often the goals of the local church for Christian growth are the antithesis of what the Bible actually teaches because of a lack of understanding of the Bible. No wonder there is so little strength and spiritual success in the local church! The pathetic fact is that many of these local churches think they are doing great! It just goes to show how little is known of what God can do when He is permitted to work!

Phase 3 of the Christian growth is the vibrant Christian's life of devotion and dedication, accepting Jesus Christ as unconditional Lord as well as Savior. It is becoming a mature Christian. "'The kingdom of heaven is like treasure hidden in a field, which a man found and covered up. Then in his joy he goes and sells all that he has and buys that field. Again, the kingdom of heaven is like a merchant in search of fine pearls, who, on finding one pearl of great value, went and sold all that he had and bought it.'" (Matthew 13:44–46). That treasure, that pearl of great price, is the vibrant Christian's life of devotion and dedication, which gives us "And the peace of God, which surpasses all understanding, will guard your hearts and your minds in Christ Jesus" (Philippians 4:7) in a satisfying personal relationship with our Lord. John 10:10b states, "I am come that they might have life and have it more abundantly."

SERVANT (VOLUNTARY SLAVE)

What does God really want for and from His people? We have gradually been getting to this last phase of the potential growth of a Christian.

The Old Testament gives us a very important picture of this last and most fruitful and fulfilling phase of being a Christian. This picture is given in three of the five books of the Pentateuch, all except Genesis and Numbers. I call this word picture the welfare system of the Hebrews, given in Exodus 21:2–6, Leviticus 25:39–43, and Deuteronomy 15:12–17. Rather than reading them all, included in the following passages is a good picture of that system.

- Leviticus 25:39–40 states, "If your brother becomes poor beside you and sells himself to you, you shall not make him serve as a slave: he shall be with you as a hired servant and as a sojourner. He shall serve with you until the year of the jubilee."

- Deuteronomy 15:12–17 states, "If your brother, a Hebrew man or a Hebrew woman, is sold to you, he shall serve you six years, and in the seventh year you shall let him go free from you. And when you let him go free from you, you shall not let him go empty-handed. You shall furnish him liberally out of your flock, out of your threshing floor, and out of your winepress. As the LORD your God has blessed you, you shall give to him. You shall remember that you were a slave in the land of Egypt, and the LORD your God redeemed you; therefore I command you this today. But if he says to you, 'I will not go out from you,' because he loves you and your household, since he is well-off with you, then you shall take an awl, and put it through his ear into the door, and he shall be your slave forever. And to your female slave you shall do the same."

It is the last part of the Deuteronomy passage that is important for this picture of this last, but very important, essential, but seldom attained potential phase of a mature Christian. If the temporary servant (slave) decides that he does not want to be set free "because he loves you and your household, since he is well-off with you," then the servant chooses to becomes a voluntary but permanent slave.

God's desire for each of us, His people, is that we, knowing growing in His love, and experiencing our vibrant, fulfilled life with Him (John 10:10b), volunteer to be His slave forever.

Both Paul and Peter wrote about being a voluntary slave to their Lord Jesus Christ. Paul, in Romans 1:1, stated, "Paul, a servant of Christ Jesus, called to be an apostle, set apart for the gospel of God." I love that he said "separated unto the Gospel of God." So should we all say. Paul's word *servant* is the Greek word transliterated *doulos*, Strong's #1401. The Greek language has several words for slave or servant. The word Paul used is the most demeaning, lowest form of slavery. This slave is so bound to his or her master that "his will being altogether consumed in the will of the of the other" [master] (*The Complete Word Study Dictionary* – New Testament, Spiros Zodhiates, TH.D, World Bible Publishers, Inc., for *doulos* [slave], page 483, Iowa Falls, Iowa, June 1992); "metaph., one who gives himself up to another's will, those whose service is used by Christ in extending and advancing his cause among men" (Online Bible, Ver. 5.10.00.03, June 25, 2016, Online Bible Foundation, Online Bible Greek Lexicon, Copyrighted by Larry Pierce on Strong's #1401). This is exactly what the Christian in the fourth phase of the walk with the Lord is learning, but voluntarily instead of forcibly! Paul used the same word in Titus 1:1. Peter used the same word in Second Peter 1:1. Do you think that it is a coincidence that the two people mentioned most in the book of Acts, as workers in the Gospel, have said this same thing? No, I don't think so. Do you think God put these three passages, along with the Old Testament picture, in the Bible so we should learn from them? Absolutely!

This is what Peter was writing about in Second Peter 1:2–4. God gave us, in this passage, the "how" to be God's voluntary slave.

"Simon Peter, a servant and apostle of Jesus Christ, To those who have obtained a faith of equal standing with ours by the righteousness of our God and Savior Jesus

Christ: May grace and peace be multiplied to you in the *knowledge* of God and of Jesus our Lord. His divine power has granted to us all things that pertain to life and godliness, through the *knowledge* of him who called us to his own glory and excellence, by which he has granted to us his precious and very great promises, so that through them you may become partakers of the divine nature, having escaped from the corruption that is in the world because of sinful desire."

The key word in this passage quoted from Second Peter 1 is *knowledge*, transliterated *epignosis*, Strong's #1922 in verses 2 and 3, which means to have a very precise, correct, personal, intimate, experiential understanding, and vibrant life relationship with our Lord. It is the body of knowledge that we have received by experience, perception, understanding, seeing, and reasoning. The verb form is very similar, *epiginosko*, Strong #1922. Zodhiates (ibid, pg 624) gives us a very good and usable defines *epiginosis*.

"It is more intensive than *gnosis* (1108), knowledge, because it expresses a thorough participation in the acquiring of knowledge on the part of the learner, In the NT, if often refers to knowledge which powerfully influences the form of religious life, a knowledge laying claim to personal involvement… It increases the spiritual blessings upon the believer (Ephesians 1:17; 2 Peter 1:2-3) and determines the manifestations of the religious life… [it] refers to the knowledge which enables one to avoid error."

This is the kind of knowledge that is only obtained by spending much time in the Word, letting it soak into who we are by meditation and letting it change us, along with prayer for more than a few minutes a day. It needs hours, not minutes, per week, to come to this spiritual maturity. Please note that this "knowledge" does not always come from being educated in a Bible college. It only comes from much personal time spent with our Lord, in close communion and fellowship through Bible study and through prayer. A few other passages which describe this relationship with our Lord, all containing the Greek word *epignosis*, follow. Look at the full context of each passage and how the context relates to the word *epignosis*.

- Ephesians 4:13–15 (emphasis added) states, "until we all attain to the unity of the faith and of the *knowledge* of the Son of God, to mature manhood, to the measure of the stature of the fullness of Christ, so that we may no longer be children, tossed to and fro by the waves and carried about by every wind of doctrine, by human cunning, by craftiness in deceitful schemes. Rather, speaking the truth in love, we are to grow up in every way into him who is the head, into Christ,"

- Philippians 1:9–11 (emphasis added) states, "And it is my prayer that your love may abound more and more, with *knowledge* and all discernment, so that you may approve what is excellent, and so be pure and blameless for the day of Christ, filled with the fruit of righteousness that comes through Jesus Christ, to the glory and praise of God."

- Colossians 1:9–12 states, "And so, from the day we heard, we have not ceased to pray for you, asking that you may be filled with the knowledge of his will in all spiritual wisdom and understanding, so as to walk in a manner worthy of the Lord, fully pleasing to him, bearing fruit in every good work and increasing in the knowledge of God. May you be strengthened with all power, according to his glorious might, for all endurance and patience with joy, giving thanks to the Father, who has qualified you to share in the inheritance of the saints in light."

Each passage above, along with Second Peter 1:2-4, shows the noun, *epignosis*, in a different way. Look at them and understand them. Then, read Second Peter 1:5–8, where God gives us a list of characteristics that a Christian grows into, generally one characteristic at a time, as we grow in that great, intimate, full knowledge and understanding that Second Peter 1a;2-4 promises. Then, Peter tells us, in verses 5-8, what has been and will continue to happen, saying, "For this very reason, make every effort to supplement:

"your faith with virtue,
"and virtue with knowledge,
"and knowledge with self-control,
"and self-control with steadfastness,
"and steadfastness with godliness,
"and godliness with brotherly affection,
"and brotherly affection with love.

"For if these qualities are yours and are increasing, they keep you from being ineffective or unfruitful in the knowledge of our Lord Jesus Christ. For whoever lacks these qualities is so nearsighted that he is blind, having forgotten that he was cleansed from his former sins. Therefore, brothers, be all the more diligent to make your calling and election sure, for if you practice these qualities you will never fall. For in this way there will be richly provided for you an entrance into the eternal kingdom of our Lord and Savior Jesus Christ. Therefore I intend always to remind you of these qualities, though you know them and are established in the truth that you have."

When we live as a voluntary slave to Christ, we will have total peace and joy with God, living a very fulfilled life, but more importantly, we will be doing God's will, His way, and by His timing. His will has become our will. In so doing, God gives each of us who are saved by grace, the reasons for which He created us, over and above his general purposes for us, often differing from the special purposes He gives to others. Also, God's grace, love, and Holy Spirit will be working honestly, virtuously, and without compromise within us and through us to others. What more can a Christian ask?

Many a mature Christian has said, "I am no slave," putting their meaning on what Jesus said in John 8:32: "you will know the truth, and the truth will set you free." These people have not yet reached this phase of Christian growth and maturity. Maybe they never will.

Think about the logic of this. God is very logical if we look at things the way God does (Biblical wisdom). God said, in John 10:10, "The thief comes only to steal and kill and destroy. I came that they may have life and have it abundantly." The closer we are to God in our obedience and worship, the more abundant will be our life in Christ. That means, when we so totally divorce ourselves of our self-centeredness, the more abundant our life will be. Another way to say that is, the more we are the voluntary slave to God through Christ, the more free we are to be obedient to God and live the abundant life in Him that He promised in John 10:10b, "the truth will set you free." What more can we ask?

In the devoted, or dedicated phase of being a Christian, we started to get our identity, not from being a Methodist, Presbyterian, Baptist, etc., but simply by being a Bible believing and living Christian. If this did not happen, one would not have progressed very far in that stage and is unable to enter into this final stage of being a Christian. We must transcend, rise above, these splintered divisions of the Christian existence. At the same time, we cannot compromise God's Holy Word or what we have, in Christ, become. I will add a little to this subject of ceasing to be a denomination-alist or other kind of separatist fellowship group, such as Baptist, IFCI (Independent Fundamental Church International), Pentecostal Holiness, Charismatic, Presbyterian, Methodist, etc. Several years ago, this writer coined a word that I think other Bible students of the Word also use, which is Biblicist. The term can be explained by saying that is that a Biblicist will not adhere to any man made doctrinal code or standards of belief, even those based upon the Bible (but formed and defined by man), but, only to the Bible, correctly translated and understood as God intended, according to Second Peter 1:16–21:

> For we did not follow cleverly devised myths when we made known to you the power and coming of our Lord Jesus Christ, but we were eyewitnesses of his majesty. For when he received honor and glory from God the Father, and the voice was borne to him by the Majestic Glory, "This is my beloved Son, with whom I am well pleased,"

we ourselves heard this very voice borne from heaven, for we were with him on the holy mountain. And we have something more sure, the prophetic word, to which you will do well to pay attention as to a lamp shining in a dark place, until the day dawns and the morning star rises in your hearts, knowing this first of all, that no prophecy of Scripture comes from someone's own interpretation. For no prophecy was ever produced by the will of man, but men spoke from God as they were carried along by the Holy Spirit.

In other words, God, through Peter, has told us that *the only proper use of any portion of scripture* is what the Holy Ghost intended when He gave the Word to those "*holy men of God*," which they did write, in their original writing, wrote exactly what the Holy Ghost gave them to write. Any other use of Scripture is a violation of the Scripture and hinders our knowledge of God and His Word. The beauty is that God gave us the ability, by grace alone, to understand His Word, apply it to our lives, and have fellowship with God though Jesus Christ, via His Word. It also means that we are responsible to use His Word responsibly. The violation of this is where a Christian will find those splinters (denominations and denomination-like fellowships and other man-made divisions) of the body of Christ, which are a sin against God, as well as against Christians. Wherever this author has traveled, on business or on vacation, he has found fellow Christians that believe the same thing he does. At that level, denominations are meaningless; the Bible is what binds us together, and that bond is instantaneous and firm. Unfortunately, few of those just mentioned have been pastors. It is very sad that few pastors, local church leaders, and/or administrators, ever get to this level. It comes to those who strive for that slave master relationship with Jesus Christ and His Word without the interference of man-made divisions. To get to this level, one must know and understand God's Word very well by personal study, meditation and prayer.

Let's look at the Second Peter 1:16–21 passage closely, because God is telling us something very important in it.

- Verses 16–19 state that the apostles, especially Peter, James, and John, were eyewitnesses to the glory of Jesus Christ and were students of His Word which He took care to carefully teach them, which the apostles gave to us in the New Testament, adding to the already established Old Testament. Verses 17–18 are about the transfiguration of Jesus Christ.

- Verse 20 states that *no one* has the authority to give opinion on what this or that passage means unless they are using the passage to say only what God meant it to say. That means that the Bible only must be used to interpret the Bible, using the close context, near context, greater context of chapter and / or book, dispensational understanding and the total context of the complete Word, all understood as God originally intended. When this is done, virtually all denominations and quasi-denominations (fellowships, conventions, etc.) are eliminated and unity of Ephesians 4 is accomplished.

- In verse 21, Peter is saying that the Word of God given to chosen, holy men of God, was and is verbally inspired, meaning that every word in the original text is the very word given by God the Father to God the Son to God the Holy Spirit to chosen holy men of God. It was and is also, in the original text, plenary inspired, meaning that every word is exactly where it is supposed to be in the complete Word (*logos*), beginning to end. This allows no room for anyone to say that any portion of Scripture says anything other than what God intended it to say. That also puts a narrow definition to application of the Word!

Since God's Word should be the same to everyone, as it never changes in any way, why do we have so many divisions in our Christian Family of God. It is because people will not let God be God; note that letting God be God is the purest form of humility. Those people place the meaning that they want to believe on different parts of the Word. Some of that is self centeredness put forth as protection of the unbiblical traditions of the local church or denomination or fellowship ignorance forcing itself to the forefront – this does not only apply to cults, but also to denominations and fellowships laziness in the studying Scripture

All of it is the work of Satan and his demons, along with *free will,* in the spiritual battle of unrighteousness versus God's righteousness. Since God's Word should be the same to everyone, great emphasis should be made to use only the Bible versions that are the most aligned with the original texts of Scripture as the main study tool, using paraphrases along with a literal version only to help understand the literal version. A serious student should also have original language helps to aid study. If the original languages were fully translated into English or other language, the Bible would contain several times more pages than we now have. There is that much that can be added to learned by referring to helps in the original text (Hebrew, Chaldee and Greek).

The unity of Christ's people mentioned in Ephesians 4 was previously mentioned. The body of Christ is very fractured now and has been ever since the apostolic age. Paul said, in Second Timothy 4:16, that all had forsaken him. Satan and his demons are alive and well in the body of Christ, including in the pastorate and local fellowship boards. God has beseeched us, begged us, through Paul in Ephesians 4, to have unity among the brethren of the body of Christ. True unity is the total absence of denominational / fellowship / convention group differences or divisions. True unity is the absence of the erroneous attitude of "I think it means this or that." It is total unity in the Gospel of Christ the way God intended and desires. God could have made us robots who would all agree on Biblical doctrine and application and live in unity. But He gave us freewill, so that each one of us, by his or her own conscious decision, would hopefully choose to be voluntary slaves to Him. It is only when we, by submission though grace by faith, have that Godly urge and desire to fully please our loving Lord by loving Him enough to give up ourselves as slaves, willing to take God's will as our own, that we can have that kind of unity in the body of Christ.

If you abide in me, and my words abide in you, ask whatever you wish, and it will be done for you. By this my

199

Father is glorified, that you bear much fruit and so prove to be my disciples. As the Father has loved me, so have I loved you. Abide in my love. If you keep my commandments, you will abide in my love, just as I have kept my Father's commandments and abide in his love. These things I have spoken to you, that my joy may be in you, and that your joy may be full. This is my commandment, that you love one another as I have loved you. Greater love has no one than this, that someone lays down his life for his friends. You are my friends if you do what I command you. No longer do I call you servants, for the servant does not know what his master is doing; but I have called you friends, for all that I have heard from my Father I have made known to you (John 15:7–15).

When we become voluntary slaves of Christ, out of our love for Him, He no longer calls us His servants (slaves) but calls us His friends. This is when we get, by diligently study, into that *epignosis* understanding. It is then that He blesses us with the full blessing of His fellowship. Please note that it is only when we are voluntary slaves of His that He says that He now calls us friends; when we get proud and start believing that we are past being voluntary slaves, we are no longer in that close, intimate fellowship of obedience with Him. May that desire to be voluntary slaves to Him be the great desire of all of His people. Along with the other factors of a lively, Biblical local church fellowship, it takes the working of God's motivational gifts of Romans 12 to make this come about.

When a Christian enters into stage 4, the slave of Christ, he or she will see that many passages of the Bible, especially in the New Testament, have a new and more complete and full meaning than he or she had ever known before. As he or she lives this life of being a voluntary slave to God, he or she will see that whatever doctrinal statement they held before was very inadequate and, depending upon the fellowship or denominational leadership either very, very wrong or somewhat wrong. *None are totally correct!* None are totally free from the input of mankind, replacing, to some extent, God's intended meaning. Some had picked up and kept error from the Post-Apostolic days, which were full of error, even though other doctrine is correct. Others have picked up more modern errror. God will lead His voluntary slave to the point where he or she cannot identify with that old denominational life any more, although some will find that there is not a better place to fellowship than where they are now, in spite of its inadequacies. But the personal identity will become, "I am a Bible believing and living Christian." The personal identity will not be, cannot be, "I am a" Presbyterian, Methodist, Pentecostal, Assemblies, Baptist, etc.

The real difference between the third phase of Christian growth (which I called the devotion/dedication phase) and the servant / slave phase is where the focus of the Christian's life is. In the devotion / dedication phase, the Christian is learning to see the world in the Christian worldview and asking God to be with us as we live our lives as we think we should, but leaning on the denomination / convention / fellowship doctrine. Most people in this phase, including most local church administrators, really think that they are serving God to the best of one's abilities, and maybe they are, often because of willful ignorance. That is because they had never come to understand that God has something better, and that something better is to be the joyful, fulfilled, slave of God, not living simply to be the best that we can be, but actually living out Galatians 2:20, "I have been crucified with Christ. It is no longer I who live, but Christ who lives in me. And the life I now live in the flesh I live by faith in the Son of God, who loved me and gave himself for me." Being *crucified with Christ* means to live by the will of God rather than by self will.

Paul, in his second letter to the Corinthians, wrote, "We want you to know, brothers, about the grace of God that has been given among the churches of Macedonia,…and this, not as we expected, but they gave themselves first to the Lord and then by the will of God to us" (Second Corinthians 8:1,5). This passage, which Paul used as an example to the church in Corinth, shows people who, by grace, had totally given themselves to the Lord, being effectively voluntary slaves of our Lord in their giving for the benefit of the Christians in Jerusalem. The church at Corinth had definitely not given themselves over to the Lord, and far, far too many Christians of today have never given themselves over to our LORD in that way.

Many, many years ago, as God was bringing this author out of the second phase of Christianity, into the third phase, I found Matthew 11:28–30. God drew my attention to that passage so greatly that I memorized it and have kept it in my mind's treasury ever since, "Come to me, all who labor and are heavy laden, and I will give you rest. Take my yoke upon you, and learn from me, for I am gentle and lowly in heart, and you will find rest for your souls. For my yoke is easy, and my burden is light." Just what did Jesus mean when He says that He was "meek and lowly in heart?" Obviously, "lowly in heart" means humility. But what kind of humility does He mean?

When thinking of Jesus Christ and humility, I first think of Philippians 2:6–8, "who, though he was in the form of God, did not count equality with God a thing to be grasped, but made himself nothing, taking the form of a servant, being born in the likeness of men. And being found in human form, he humbled himself by becoming obedient to the point of death, even death on a cross." This passage describes the humility of Jesus and also tells us why He was humble. His humility was being obedient, letting God the Father be God. Jesus became humble so that He would be sacrificed in great suffering and death on the cross, for our sakes. John 15:13 states, "Greater love has no one than this, that someone lays down his life for his friends." As mentioned near the beginning of this chapter, the greatest form of love is *agape* love, the love that Jesus Christ demonstrated by offering Himself as the final and perfect Passover Lamb. *Agape* love is sacrificial love, giving up a part of self in time, goods, money, and so on, to draw another to Christ or closer to Christ. This is true humility. Humility is very simply being submissive to God, doing His will, emptying ourselves of our self-will, knowing that it is Him in us that does the work. This must also preclude that we are not to consider ourselves better or more important than others.

Meekness is very often described as "gentle," which is often misunderstood as "weakness." The word, in the Old Testament and the New, has nothing to do with being weak. Conversely, meekness is great strength. It is accurately described as the gentleness of a trained horse and was used in the Greek that way. But what most people either don't know, have forgotten or ignored is that a horse, in years past, was not a pet to be ridden for exercise and enjoyment, or for entertainment, like today. A horse was a work animal. Most often, in the Bible days, it was a war animal (read Job 39:19-25). A warhorse was not gentle when used in war. A warhorse was used to charge through the enemy, causing havoc and fear, often slaughtering more of the enemy than the rider. But! When not in warfare, the horse had to be gentle to be ridden without slaughtering noncombatants, and be gentle in the stable so that the stable and other animals were not destroyed or driven away. A better definition, often used by well trained Christians, is that meekness is *strength under control.* That control is gentleness in a way that does not cause undue distress. The Bible gives a true story of Jesus and a Roman centurion with a sick servant which is a great illustration for meekness.

> When he entered Capernaum, a centurion came forward to him, appealing to him, "Lord, my servant is lying paralyzed at home, suffering terribly." And he said to him, "I will come and heal him." But the centurion replied, "Lord, I am not worthy to have you come under my roof, but only say the word, and my servant will be healed. For I too am a man under authority, with soldiers under me. And I say to one, 'Go,' and he goes, and to another, 'Come,' and he comes, and to my servant, 'Do this,' and he does it." When Jesus heard this, he marveled and said to those who followed him, "Truly, I tell you, with no one in Israel have I found such faith" (Matthew 8:5–10).

This centurion did not just have great faith and wisdom, he understood the position of Jesus Christ as God. In other words, he understood that Jesus did what God the Father told him to do, and because He was obedient to the Father, had great authority Himself from the Father. The centurion voiced his understanding by voicing his own obedience and authority, having authority over the soldiers under his authority because he was obedient to his superiors, the authority over him. This is exactly what meekness is.

We, as servants, slaves, of Jesus Christ, having taken His will as our own will, being obedient to God, are to be humble and meek. That means that:

First, we are submissive to God; John 15:7&10 states, "If you abide in me, and my words abide in you, ask whatever you wish, and it will be done for you... If you keep my commandments, you will abide in my love, just as I have kept my Father's commandments and abide in his love."

Second, we must not think of ourselves as being better than others because we are controlled, not by ourselves but by God, as the warhorse is controlled by its rider. Romans 12:3 tells us, "For by the grace given to me I say to everyone among you not to think of himself more highly than he ought to think, but to think with sober judgment, each according to the measure of faith that God has assigned.". It also means that we have great authority in the Word and ministry in the way we interact with others because we are under His authority while doing His work and will. This is most effectively done using the spiritual gifts God has gifted each believer. God works tremendously through the humility, meekness, and use of the motivational spiritual gifts of grace that He gave us! When we look at humility and meekness as described here, they work with each other, interacting with each other, making one impossible without the other. They are complementary to each other. They, when founded upon the doctrine of the Word of God, form the power that God wants to work in and through us, and He most often does this through the working of the motivational gifts He has given.

In the third possible phase of Christian life were found some examples of the way that God can and will work through His people who are submitted to Him. Following are some examples of the way God can and will work through His people who are voluntary slaves of His:

- As the corporate engineer for a large company, you are in a plant in a different state. There are a couple of fellow Christians who, like you, were beyond creeds, denominations, or denomination-like fellowships or conventions in their relationship with our God through faith, grace, the Bible, prayer, meditation and the work of the Holy Spirit. One was the Quality Engineer. One evening, after working twelve hours that day, the Christian Quality Engineer, one of Plant Engineers and yourself were left in the plant and getting ready to call it a night. The two of you knew that the plant engineer, who was half Jewish, was not saved. You say to the Quality Engineer, "Let's ask him to meet us in your office to relax and talk, then share the Gospel with him." He came, and you started talking about something to make everyone feel at ease. Then you took a breath to start to share the gospel. At that very moment, an extremely noticeable entity, a presence, an energy, came into the room, not noticed by the plant engineer. Your insides just about explode with joy, and you say silently, "Here we go, Lord!" and you start to discuss the plant engineer's Jewish heritage, starting with the Old Testament, and how Jesus Christ was the anticipated Messiah who was prophesied, giving Bible passages to support what you were sharing, then getting into the Gospel. You knew the Quality Engineer was praying the whole time. You could see the plant engineer absorbing God's Word and figuratively see the gears moving in his head while he thought on what you have said and really seemed to understand. You asked if he was ready to accept Jesus Christ as his Savior. Part of him really wanted to, but his pride (freewill) kept him from it, and he said, "No," and left the room. At the very moment that he said, "No," that entity, that presence, that energy, left the room, too. *Wow!* The Quality Engineer and you looked at each other with eyes wide open and each said, "Did you feel that?" You both did. As far as you know, the plant engineer never did surrender to Jesus Christ. But God gave him every opportunity that night.

- Fairly late one evening, you and your wife were traveling through the country toward your home from the big city.

You were both tired and eager to get home to be with your children and to get some sleep. You felt the urge to go the house of a Christian family whose wife was a good friend of your wife. It was out of the way and it was really too late to visit, being around eleven that evening. This sidelined trip was totally out of character for you to think of. You told your wife. She said, "No, it is too late and we need to get home." You said, "We are going!" You arrived at the friend's house. That family had a baby who was just beginning to walk. This baby had opened the diaper pail, in which were dirty cloth diapers soaking in water. She leaned over and fell into the diaper pail head first and drowned. Soon after, they found her, just before you and your wife got there, about twenty minutes after you had received that urge to go. This meant that your urge to go was long before the drowning had occurred. The child's parents were totally petrified with fear for this child's life, as they lived way out in the country, too far to call an ambulance to come out and with no near neighbors to call to stay with their other children while they raced to the hospital with the drowned child. That was exactly the time that you and your wife arrived. *Wow!* The parents were able to get the child to the hospital while you and your wife stayed with the family's young children. The baby was given proper treatment at the hospital and was saved, just because you paid attention to and acted upon that urge.

Those are just a couple of examples of how God's can work through a voluntary slave. These examples are truly miraculous. They are minor compared to the way God has always intended to work through you and me! For God to use you like that, you have to do what it takes, become a slave to God, no matter what anyone else thinks or says! It is a way of life commitment.

As we get near to the end of this study, let's look at 2 Chronicles 17:16, where the writer lists Jehoshaphat's mighty men, "And next to him was Amasiah the son of Zichri, who willingly offered himself unto the LORD..." (KJV). The tense of this passage, in Hebrew, is *hithpael participle*. This tense means *reflexive action*; that Amasiah had a very good reason for willingly offering himself unto the LORD. Participle means that he did this in "unbroken continuity."

The Bible does not give the reason for the reflexive action of Amasiah, why he had willingly offered himself to the Lord in unbroken continuity. I have to believe that it was because Amasiah spent quality time with the Lord in prayer, Scripture and meditation, and God blessed him for that. The Hebrew text leads us to believe that Amasiah's worship and his receiving blessings went on in a continuous cycle of greater intensity, leading to worship and more and more blessings from the Lord in each level of intensity, all resulting in Amasiah's continuous offer of himself to the Lord, being a voluntary slave of our Lord. We can learn a lot from Amasiah. If we don't have that continuing reflexive attitude of thankfulness and desire to do God's will, offering ourselves as a voluntary servant to the Lord, we don't know God well enough through His Word and through what He wants to do in and through us.

None of us are perfect. Because we are not perfect, there will be some fluidity in the last three phases. As people gain phases three and four, they may, and most likely will, have a relapse and slip down a notch or two. That happens. The key is to keep from staying down that notch or two. God is faithful and has already supplied grace if we are willing to use it.

The question comes up, "Why haven't I realized all of this before?" The answer may be that, in most conservative church congregations or fellowships, the focus is on getting people saved along with a separatist doctrine. That focus is not what God wants for the local church. The focus that God wants for the local church is, of course, worship and fellowship, encouraging, exhorting, and uplifting others, but also learning more about Him and exercising our spiritual gifts. When those things come to the forefront, the salvation of souls comes pretty automatically as we go about our daily lives, which is where God wants it. As most worship now exists, a few people minister to most of the people. This is very wrong. The few people end up controlling what they think should happen; too often what some of the few think should happen is to protect their own positions by keeping the most from getting very active. Recognize what David said in Psalm 119:10-11, 99-100, "With my whole heart I seek you; let me not wander from your commandments! I have stored up your word in my heart, that I might not sin against you… I have more understanding than all my teachers, for your testimonies are my meditation. I understand more than the aged, for I keep your precepts." Reading Psalm 119 often is an excellent way to keep our mind and attitude in tune with God and His Word. This continuing to be a slave of Christ can be accomplished, by God's grace and by our own efforts of time spent in the Bible, meditating what we have learned so that it becomes a part of us, and prayer. Have that *reflexive continuing* attitude of Amasiah.

Many people, over many years, have found that exciting fourth phase and have written hymns about the life of the voluntary slave of Christ. God had the song "At the Cross" going through this author's head a couple of days before these last words were written.

Alas! And did my Savior bleed? And did my Sov-'reign die?
Would He devote that sacred head For such a worm as I?

Was it for crimes that I have done He groaned upon the tree?
Amazing pity! Grace unknown! And love beyond degree!

Well might the sun in darkness hide And shut his glories in,
When Christ, the mighty Maker, died For man the creature's sin.

But drops of grief can ne'er repay The debt of love I owe;
Here, Lord, I give myself away – 'Tis all that I can do!

Chorus:
At the cross, at the cross where I first saw the light,
And the burden of my heart rolled away,
It was there by faith I received my sight,
And now I am happy all the day!

There are many hymns with a similar message, such as "Take My Life and Let It Be," "I Surrender All," and "Only One Life." The hymns mentioned above are just a few of the many with a similar message. Don't neglect the old hymns.

A passage to close with, from that great Psalms about the Word (*logos*) of God about *rhemas* is:

Teach me, O LORD, the way of your statutes; and I will keep it to the end.

> 34 Give me understanding, that I may keep your law and observe it with my whole heart.
>
> 35 Lead me in the path of your commandments, for I delight in it.
>
> 36 Incline my heart to your testimonies, and not to self-ish gain!
>
> 37 Turn my eyes from looking at worthless things; and give me life in your ways.
>
> 38 Confirm to your servant your promise, that you may be feared.
>
> 39 Turn away the reproach that I dread, for your rules are good.
>
> 40 Behold, I long for your precepts; in your righteous-ness give me life!
>
> 41 Let your steadfast love come to me, O LORD, your salvation according to your promise;
>
> 42 then shall I have an answer for him who taunts me, for I trust in your word.
>
> 43 And take not the word of truth utterly out of my mouth, for my hope is in your rules.
>
> 44 I will keep your law continually, forever and ever,
>
> 45 and I shall walk in a wide place, for I have sought your precepts.
>
> (Psalms 119:33–45)

ABOUT THE AUTHOR

Although Larry had received Jesus Christ as his Savior at a young age, the church denomination that the family belonged to was fairly liberal and was getting more and more liberal, although Larry did not realize it for many years. Discipleship was nonexistent. The salvation message was not real important, and a vibrant Christian life was not taught. After Larry got married and started to have children, he became more and more interested in the Bible. He became more and more drawn to his Lord and, in his early thirties, had the thought come into his head, "Larry, you are sitting on the fence, get off on one side or the other." Larry knew that this was about his compromised Christian life. Because God had been working on him, it was very easy for him to get off the fence on God's side.

Larry realized that he was pretty much a fool and prayed to his Lord, "God, I know that some of what I have been taught in church is good and right, but I also know that some of what I have learned is not right." He said to his Lord, "I don't want to try to sift the good from the bad, I want to start over learning of You and your Word, and, God, I want you to teach me!" And God did start teaching him, some of it through godly pastors, and much of it by intently studying the Bible. Immediately, Larry felt a heavy but wonderful burden that lead to studying the Bible deeply, many, many hours a week, for several years.

After about three years of deep study, he realized that he was learning so much that it had to come out. Jeremiah, in chapter 20:9, said that he was not going to speak for God any more, as he landed in trouble more and more, "But his word was in mine heart as a burning fire shut up in my bones, and I was weary with forbearing, and I could not stay." Larry can testify, not to wanting to break away from God, but to God's Word burning in his heart so that he cannot keep silent. By this time, Larry had realized that the church denomination of his heritage was no longer a place that he and his family could remain. His goal, from then on, was to be a vibrant part of the most biblically conservative local church that he could find.

It was during this time that Larry also felt the burden to work in the local church to help people grow in spiritual maturity, coming to know God and His Word abundantly and having a wonderful personal relationship with Him.

Although numerous people had told Larry that he should be a pastor, Larry never felt that desire. He is a teacher, not a pastor; he had never been in a full-time position of ministry but has been in the full-time labor as a servant of his God for over thirty years. He has been retired for several years and works part-time in a toy store.

Printed in May 2019
by Rotomail Italia S.p.A., Vignate (MI) - Italy